Praise for
Finding a Better Version of You Through Franchising

"Franchising is one of the most powerful pathways to achieve your dreams. To truly understand if franchising is right for you and how to most efficiently and effectively get the results and rewards you desire and deserve, read Rich's excellent analysis, guide and companion on "Finding a Better Version of You Through Franchising"."

>Don Marks,
>Creator of Brands, Consultant, CEO, and Owner, The Pro Network Brands (Pop-A-Lock, TemperaturePro, PlumbingPro and ElectricPro)

"Finding a Better Version of You Through Franchising" is very thorough and will provide any future business owner with everything they need to know to evaluate, buy, and operate a franchised business successfully. There's a lot of great information here and that goes broad and deep on topics."

>Rob Weddle
>Chief Executive Officer, The Authority Brands (The Cleaning Authority, Homewatch CareGivers, America's Swimming Pool Co., Mosquito Squad, Benjamin Franklin Plumbing, Mister Sparky Electric and One Hour Heating & Air Conditioning)

"A great read for anyone interested in learning about franchising. Rich describes the landscape, the motives and the goals of both the franchise system and the local franchise owner. He gives honest, practical insights which can be used throughout the readers franchise journey. Rich is a great businessman whose insights are regularly sought after in the franchise community. This book contains many of those great insights for would-be franchise owners."

Sabrina Wall
Founder and CEO, Franchise Brokers Association (FBA)

"I highly recommend working with Rich Greer. I have had the pleasure of working with Rich and interacting with him one-on-one numerous times. He is extremely knowledgeable and very professional. If you are looking to buy a business or franchise I would strongly encourage working with Rich and reading his book, he is one of the best in the business!"
Don Daszkowski
Founder, International Franchise Professionals Group (IFPG.org)

"Rich really understands - first hand - what it means to become a franchisee, work in a system with great success and now be able to expertly guide his clients to make a decision to benefit their lives and the lives of their loved ones. This is a well-presented explanation of the franchise discovery and in my opinion - an excellent assessment of how to overcome the inherent FEAR that keeps people from pursuing their dreams of business ownership. Highly recommended reading."
Dan Durney
Franchise Development Director, FranMaster

"When I left my corporate life after twenty years and became an entrepreneur, I discovered an amazing method to be successful --- franchising! Rich Greer gives you a thorough understanding of franchising in "Finding a Better Version of You Through Franchising". I enjoyed Rich's take on the franchisee-franchisor relationship, which is the key to a franchise's long-term success. Honest and insightful, this book is an absolute must-read for anyone who is exploring alternatives for small business ownership."

Curt M. Maier
Vetrepreneur, two-time franchisee and currently Vice President of Business Development for International Business Associates (IBA), the oldest M&A/Business Brokerage in the Pacific Northwest.

Finding a Better Version of You Through Franchising

Finding a Better Version of You Through Franchising

Defining what franchising is all about and to help you determine if it is the right fit in order to find a better version of you.

By

Rich Greer

Finding a Better Version of You Through Franchising

Copyright © 2020 by Rich Greer

Printed in the United States of America

ISBN: 9781654594206

DEDICATION

I dedicate this book to everyone looking to find a better version of themselves and to those exploring franchising as a means of meeting their professional, financial and lifestyle goals. I sincerely hope that this book will help in guiding you toward your true purpose in life.

ACKOWLEDGEMENTS

I would like to express my special thanks to my wife of 37 years, Barbara Greer, and very good friend Dan Durney for the hundreds of hours each devoted to editing and re-editing this book again and again. Without their dedication and encouragement "Finding a Better Version of You Through Franchising" would never have been written.

Table of Contents

Table of Contents

Table of Contents

Table of Contents

Table of Contents

Table of Contents

Introduction

 In 1988 two important events occurred in my life. First was the birth of my one and only child, my son Michael. The second event was my discovery and newly formed interest in the franchising business model.

My road to franchising began when I received a coupon in the mail from Jiffy Lube. My car needed an oil change, so I drove over (living in Boulder, CO at the time) and met the owner. As I was waiting for the technicians to finish with my car I started a conversation with him. He told me, among other things, that he owned the other three Jiffy Lubes in Boulder. I became very interested in this – how could a guy with limited experiences become the owner of four quick lube service centers? I asked if I could come in the next Saturday and stay the day with him. Since by this time we had become friends he agreed. I brought in breakfast for everyone and enjoyed the day. I did a mental count of the cars that came in. That evening I took out my calculator (this was before PCs and spreadsheets) and did some quick math – the number of vehicles in that day times the average charge,

Introduction

times 30 days, minus lease payments, COGS, labor, etc. Then I multiplied that number by 4 (the number of stores he owned) then multiplied that by 12 (months in the year). There I was staring at what should be his approximate net profit. Look at all those zeros and commas! I was hooked. The next year my family and I moved to the Houston TX suburbs and I purchased two territories in a maid service franchise. Quickly my franchise rose to be in the top 2% of franchise sales in a franchise system with over 1,500 franchisees. Nine years later the home office asked several of their top offices if they wanted to sell. They offered much more than I thought it was worth and it was a cash offer. Two months later I was standing in a parking lot holding a check with my name on it. Look at all those zeros and commas! I took off the next two years to see where I would land next. After a two-year vacation it was time to go back to work. In 2001 I purchased a territory in a senior care franchise. Again, within a couple of years I was in the top 2% of office sales. Seven years later the son of one of my clients offered to purchase the business, again a cash deal. By now I had identified myself as a serial entrepreneur. Within two months again I was standing in a parking lot looking at a check made out to me. Look at all those zeros and commas - again! How lucky I was, having chosen two great franchises. I later learned that it indeed was all luck. With over 4,500 franchised brands it would have been very easy to have found the wrong brand for me. What I learned is that, like everything else in life, nothing is perfect for any one person. What appeals to one person would make someone else hold their nose. After selling my last franchise I decided that I wanted to give back to franchising – I felt a sense of duty to help others manage the due diligence when choosing a franchise for them. In 2011 I became a franchise broker. Using my thirty years' experience coupled with a well-defined process I have since helped hundreds of people find their perfect franchise.

Finding a Better Version of You Through Franchising

Most people whom I come across tell me that yes, they want to explore what franchising may provide for them and their families, but they have no idea where to start. You may be overwhelmed with over 4,500 franchise options. I'm confident I can help.

The purpose of this book is to inform the reader about what franchising is and what it is not. You will learn the ins and outs of franchising, the terms, legal and regulatory items. We will also delve into how my clients deal with that biggest concern – _F E A R_. When you encounter that beast just remember, what are you fearful of? The unknown? If so, then would you agree that the best way to eliminate that fear is to get information – and a lot of it? Then you are able to make any determinations based on facts, not emotions. In short, this book is written for you, the franchise candidate, who needs assistance from someone who is impartial, has over 30 years' experience in the franchising industry and thus knows what to look for and what to avoid, understands that _you are only learning, not buying_ and works for you, his client. Enjoy the book and if ever I can be of assistance to you, please contact me. My contact information is on the last page of this book. Please feel free to reach out to me for more information.

The author does recommend that you read this book from the first chapter through the last chapter in sequence in order to better absorb the content. However, each chapter does stand on its own so the reader can skip any chapter and go to those the reader finds most important. Happy reading!

Introduction

Rich Greer, President
Nations Franchise Source

History and Growth of Franchising

What is a franchise?

Franchising is not a business unto itself. It is a business expansion strategy. That's a significant distinction that is not always clear. McDonalds is in the fast food business, they are not in the business of franchising. Ramada is in the business of operating properties. Snap-On Tools is in the business of selling tools. These businesses chose the franchising model for their expansion plan. Franchising is nothing more than a business model these businesses (and others) use for local, state wide, national and worldwide expansion.

Franchising is an incredible opportunity when it is done well. For a person looking to move up into the upper middle classes, it is the opportunity for wealth creation through the ownership of their own business. For our youth, it is the opportunity to get a first-rung job, gain experience in the workplace and have independently earned money in their pockets. For older or more experienced workers it is an opportunity to advance their management skills and start their own businesses. This is their opportunity to be the President and CEO of their own organization. For the investor and investor groups, franchising provides an executive model that provides a semi-passive business (the semi-passive model is explained in a later chapter) with a long-term and handsome return. For the consumer, it is the assurance that when they make their purchasing decision, they can do so with confidence trusted knowing that it is their trusted neighbor who owns the business.

Take the opportunity to understand what franchising is all about. It is the most effective and productive way the "Great American Dream" of independent business ownership is being achieved every day in the United States.

Given its long history in the United States and its importance to our overall economy it is surprising how misunderstood franchising seems to be with the general public and with government officials. Franchising is merely the partnering of a brand between two independent companies: One company has an opportunity to offer and the other makes the investment in that opportunity by developing their own locally-owned business.

History of franchising

Globally

The first examples of franchising as a way of doing business are found in early eighteenth century Germany, where brewers set up contracts with tavern owners to sell their beer exclusively in the taverns.

Nationally

Franchising in the United States goes all the way back to Benjamin Franklin. Franklin started a small chain of printing shops and newspapers in the Colonies and signed his first franchise agreement on September 13, 1731 with Thomas Whit Marsh for a printing shop in Charleston, South Carolina. Franklin's third franchise was with

Finding a Better Version of You Through Franchising

Elizabeth Timothy, who published the South Carolina Gazette and is recognized as our first female newspaper publisher, remarkable for those times.

What Mr. Franklin did back then was no different from what franchisors do today. He provided his apprentices and others with an opportunity to own their businesses by giving them the training, the equipment, and the necessary tools they required to be successful business owners. Like today, the day-to-day management of the franchised business was the sole responsibility of the local business owner, reflected in Franklin's agreement with Whit Marsh: *"That the Business of printing and the disposing of the Work printed shall be under the Care, Management and Direction of the said Thomas Whit Marsh and the working Part performed by him at his Expense."*

In the United States, the earliest example of the use of franchising for nation-wide expansion occurred in the sale of products to housewives located on the American prairie. In 1851, Isaac Singer became the first American product name franchisor when he began to sell to traveling independent salesmen the rights to sell his sewing machines to end users.

Although the Singer® Sewing Machine Company was the earliest American product name franchisor, it was relatively quickly outpaced by an even more important product name franchisor: Coca-Cola. In the early 1890s, Coca-Cola chose to franchise the rights to bottle its carbonated beverage to a large number of independent businessmen who received exclusive territories in which to distribute the product in return for paying for and assuming the risk of distributing the product.

Franchising really took off as a form of business in the 1950s and 1960s when many of the current large franchise chains, businesses such as Tastee-Freez®, KFC®, McDonald's, and Burger King® were established. The acceleration of franchising in the 1950s and 1960s can be attributed largely to two factors: the rise of television advertising and the establishment of the national highway system.

Franchising creates a reliable customer experience

After World War II, franchising exploded in the American economy after the passage of a remarkable federal law called the "Lanham Act" that allowed for the sharing of a brand so long as the brand owner controlled the quality of the products and services being delivered to the public. How franchise systems achieve consistency is of little importance to consumers; what they want when they make their purchasing decision is that the product or service they buy from any branded location is the same regardless of where they buy it. Who owns the location or who manages the business on a day-to-day basis is not important to the consumer.

The ability of franchise systems to achieve an extremely high level of consumer satisfaction, regardless of where the customer shops and regardless of who owns the business, is likely what confuses many people into thinking that local franchisees are merely managers of chain locations. Next time you are in a branded location, look for the sign that says "locally-owned and operated." You may be shopping at your neighbor's business.

Introduction of regulatory agencies – Out of the dark, into the light

Perhaps because of the growth of franchising in the 1960s, that decade witnessed the formation of a flurry of fly-by-night franchise operations that established their systems, sold them to franchisees, took the franchisees' money, and quickly shut down. The loss of many people's investment in these franchises led to the beginning of franchise regulation in the 1970s. The Federal Trade Commission (FTC) initiated its first franchise fraud investigations in 1975. In that same year, the North American Securities Administration drew up draft guidelines for Uniform Franchise Offering Circulars (UFOCs), which became the standard form for disclosing franchise opportunities to franchisees. This growing federal effort in the 1970s also culminated in the establishment of disclosure requirements and business rules for selling franchises by the FTC in 1979 and the start of the regulated era of franchising. The UFOC was revised by the FTC in July 2007 resulting in the current Franchise Disclosure Document (FDD). The FDD is a legal disclosure document that must be given to individuals interested in buying a U.S. franchise as part of the pre-sale due diligence process. It contains information essential to potential franchisees about to make a significant investment. (I have a sample copy of the FDD's Table of Contents at the end of this chapter for your review). As a result of this effort, franchising is now a regulated form of business, making an understanding of the legal environment in which it operates important to you as a franchisee. Franchising has evolved from a franchise sales focus to a franchise support focus.

How does a business become a franchise?

The typical franchisor begins as a small, locally-owned business that has achieved some success in their neighborhood. Typically they start on the path to franchising when a customer asks them how they can open a similar business. This question is often the trigger that results in new franchise systems being born. Over the next few months the local business owners will work with lawyers, consultants, accountants, bankers, web designers and other professionals to design and develop the franchise system — a considerable investment.

This investment can also be risky because no one can guarantee to the emerging franchisor that anyone will ever choose to become their franchisee, regardless of how much they have invested in developing the system.

Once the franchise system is ready the emerging franchisor will generally spend months investing in advertising and marketing to recruit their first franchisee. If they are lucky, three or four months after they start offering franchises their first franchise agreement will be signed.

How does someone become a franchisee?

For the franchisee, after two to three months of due diligence and then signing the franchise agreement the real work begins. They then begin the process of funding their new business, looking for the right location, negotiating their lease, hiring architects and builders. This also involves furnishing their location with the necessary equipment and fixtures, buying the products and supplies they will need as well as attending training at the franchisor's offices, attracting employees, training their own management and staff then marketing their new business in their neighborhood. They do it all in the expectation that customers will come through their door. The franchisor typically takes over the buildout for the new franchisee, even negotiating lease agreements. Also, many franchisors will help the new franchisee by flying out to the local franchisee's office after their corporate training, helping to open the office, interview staff with the new owner with recommendations for whom to hire, initial marketing efforts and of course to celebrate the ribbon cutting ceremony. Thankfully, sharing a brand with a recognized franchisor means they will often have customers who are already looking for that precise branded product or service even before the business is open. It is the sharing of a brand between two independent companies, with the neighborhood location owned and under the control of the franchisee, which makes franchising so successful.

Finding a Better Version of You Through Franchising

Franchises are independent businesses

My first job at the age of 15 was at a locally-owned business. Most executives begin their basic work and management skills from similar first-rung positions. Franchising has become the largest trainer of entrepreneurial skills in the United States and because of that many franchises today are owned by individuals who started their careers working at entry-level positions in locally-owned franchised operations.

From a practical point of view, the role of a franchisor is to grow their number of franchises and to support those franchised businesses before and after they are open. The role of the franchisee is to serve the public branded products and services in their local markets to the quality standards as defined by the franchisor; the franchisee has control over the day-to-day management of their business, including their employees.

Both the franchisor and franchisee are independent businesses — the only real control that a franchisor has over its franchisees is ensuring that the system's shared brand experience is delivered at the same level of quality that consumers expect and the law requires. The power of franchising is that over the years we have learned how to share a brand and achieve the goal of consistent sustainability by allowing independent business people to own and manage a business and in the process create for themselves wealth and vital local employment opportunities.

Thriving locally-owned businesses today have created the most successful growth in the middle class than at any time in history. Because of franchising, local wealth is created in communities. Solid careers are born because of the skills learned in first-rung positions that can evolve into management or even franchise ownership. Consider that if you work for a non-franchised company, the chance that you can ever own a location under that brand is zero. But for workers at a franchised location, that ownership goal is achieved every day in the United States.

How big is franchising?

Small business is a pretty broad term. The United States Small Business Administration (SBA) defines it as any company with less than 500 employees. The country has roughly 30.2 million small businesses employing 58.9 million people according to the SBA. Companies with less than 100 employees actually employ the majority of workers working at a small business.

There are nearly 850,000 franchise establishments in more than 120 industries employing over 9 million people in the United States alone. Franchising is the dominant creator of small independently-owned businesses in the United States and has been for decades. Even during the most recent recession, while other business models contracted, franchising continued to expand, creating economic opportunities for new business owners and leading the nation in job creation.

Franchising has immeasurably improved our quality of life, and likely a day not will go by where the average American will not find the opportunity to shop at a locally-owned franchise. Consumers appreciate that while the products and services they purchase are brand quality, the local business owners are their neighbors attending the same houses of worship, sponsoring the same local events, having kids in the same schools, and caring like any resident about the quality of life in their community.

Why has franchising seen so much growth in recent years?

When this nation was founded most families were entrepreneurial, using personal skills and interests to make a living. Early Americans were either a:

- Farmer

Finding a Better Version of You Through Franchising

- Proprietor
- Manufacturer
- Blacksmith
- Brewer
- Tailor/Seamstress

There were very few employees. At this point in time, ours was a local-agricultural economy. Business owners had few and limited distribution systems. We had no railroads or refrigeration. Business owners sold their products and services to the local communities.

But that changed in the late 19th and early 20th centuries as our nation rose from an agriculture economy to an industrial economy. More and more people left the farm to work in the cities to make a better and stable living. Better distribution systems were available. Railcars were refrigerated starting in 1867. We had trans-American railroad available to ship goods across the country in 1869. By 1920, more Americans lived in cities than in rural areas for the first time in US history. This rolled us from a local-agricultural economy into a national-industrial economy.

Then, around the late 1960s to mid-1970s we moved from a national economy to a worldwide economy. Overseas shipping and labor became plentiful and cheap; however, the corporate structure and monolithic "old school" systems of the industrial age began to crumble. We saw many jobs and much manufacturing leave this country to be replaced with companies in countries offering much cheaper labor. Fierce competition forced companies to outsource labor and material purchases as much as possible in order to offer a competitive price to the consumer. This change did as it was intended and now the consumer has many options at fair prices. However, we saw many manufacturing jobs go overseas. Those jobs are lost forever. Many people experienced layoffs as a result. Now, instead of getting a job right out of college and retiring from that job forty years later we see the average wage earners have 6-8 job changes and 3 changes in professions (per a recent Department of Labor (DOL) report).

Unintentional age discrimination that people over 45 often experience has made changing positions much harder, especially as you earn a higher salary. That same DOL report shows that statistically the odds are not in your favor of finding a job quickly and replacing your income after you leave your position. In fact, on average Americans will be job-hunting one month for every $10,000 of income they are seeking to replace, even longer in a difficult economy. Even then the average time they can expect to hold that position is only 2-3 years and you repeat the cycle once again and again.

With the combination of unreliable job security coupled with ongoing age discrimination many of us look towards self-employment to give us our security. A recent USA Today article states that "Three in five (62 percent) Americans want to make their dream of owning a business a reality."

Reasons to start your own business

When thinking about the reasons to start a company, current business owners say the yearning for a better lifestyle trumps the desire to make more money. The ability to be in charge of your own destiny and work flexibly were the top reasons existing owners provided, followed by financial independence, added satisfaction and improved work/life balance.

Similarly, aspiring entrepreneurs cite the lure of being in charge of their own destiny as the number one appeal of owning a business. A recent Inc.com article shows that the prospect of making more money was the fifth cited reason for those who have yet to make their business a reality.

Finding a Better Version of You Through Franchising

Top ten reasons to run your own business

1. You control your own destiny.
2. You are seeking freedom.
3. You can find your own unique work/lifestyle balance.
4. You can follow your passion.
5. You create a legacy income.
6. You take the risk, you reap the entire reward
7. You choose the people with whom you want to work.
8. You can challenge yourself.
9. You can give back to your community.
10. You can feel pride in building something of your own.

<u>Why are people holding back?</u>

But not everyone is attracted to being an entrepreneur. There are many reasons why an individual does not pursue the dream of becoming an entrepreneur. Some are legitimate reasons, including the fact that personal desires and dreams do not include being in business for yourself. Some people simply do not have a desire to be in business for themselves and that is perfectly legitimate. It is interesting to note that a recent survey showed that over 70% of those interviewed indicated that they had a desire to own a business and yet most of these people will never do it. Sometimes financial constraints or personal and family reasons are the inhibitors that simply will not allow for the beginning of a new venture.

Not everyone who wants to open a small business does. The reasons vary among those who admit the desire, but the top two fears are:

1. The financial commitment required to open the business
2. Fear of failure

We discuss these concerns and others in a later chapter.

History and Growth of Franchising

Sample FDD Table of Contents

The Insecurity of Job Security

Over the last several decades we have looked backed to our grandparents, parents, and in many cases even our own life experiences and have been given the impression that a job means security and if we become better educated and work hard that our careers and incomes will continue to advance as we grow older. However, the changing trends and facts may be quite different than our perception.

For those of us who have been analyzing the facts there seems to be definite growing signs of "ageism" and growing forms of age discrimination. Whatever our age, many are committed to believing those issues are happening to others or that it occurs to people five years older from whatever age that we currently are. The facts strongly suggest that's an unrealistic measurement tool. The real facts (according to at least two independent state studies) suggest that age discrimination starts at age 45! Much lower than what many are willing to admit. The consequence of not recognizing the trends can be and has become very costly for many.

The Insecurity of Job Security

Here are disturbing figures:

- People past the age of 45 looking for a new job can often take twice as long (or longer) to find a job versus younger age groups.
- Many employers are less likely to interview and hire people that are currently unemployed.
- There are often three people applying for every new job (many times those other candidates are younger and cheaper).
- Length of replacement jobs are frequently shorter than previously held jobs (typical average is 2 ½ years for people past the age of 45). Once you lose that job you are now even older and competing with even younger competitors for the next job.
- We are seeing peak incomes declining once one passes the age of 45 (not unusual for many to see their income decrease 20-30% _IF_ one finds a job). We are simply not seeing our incomes continue to rise as our experience grows. Many times just the opposite is happening.

One would think that knowledge and experience are extremely valuable and that years of experience would be worth acquiring and keeping. So why are the trends suggesting older experience employees are not as valued? The answer may be found in technology.

Why is this happening?

Simply stated, one is either an asset or a liability. Some assets provide a better return on investment and therefore are worth more. As that return on investment of the older asset decreases or other newer asset can replace that more expensive asset the value of the older asset diminishes.

Illustrations:

- The mature experienced employee is not the only source of information anymore.
- The mature experienced employee was once the "'brains" of the business and now much of that information can be stored and accessed in a computer for $1,000 versus hiring someone than may cost tens of thousands of dollars more.
- Rather than hiring a full-time experienced and expensive employee, employers can now outsource that resource need and only pay for it when they need it, often at a fraction of the cost without providing additional costly benefits such as insurance, vacation, etc.
- Information, seminars and answers are often available free via the internet. Even the federal government has agencies (SCORE, SBDC, SBA) that will provide employers free consulting services to reduce the need and expense of keeping experience and more costly employees.

Real average earnings

For someone making $75,000 per year that works 2 ½ years and then is laid off and takes a year+ to find a job (not unusual - even though many do not think that it will take that long) - one's average yearly income is really closer to $54,000.

With that being said, people are often fixed on not accepting jobs that pay them less - even though the market value of experience may be perceived as less valuable or deteriorating. One must accept that fact, re-invent themselves, or simply take their skills and knowledge and consider business ownership over the job.

How to regain control and better security

- Retrain - Reinvent yourself. This may be difficult or costly.
- Focus on careers where there is growing demand and shrinking personnel resources
- Consider business/franchise ownership

The argument for business or franchise ownership

Business ownership is one of the few areas where one can gain greater control of one's own destiny and provide greater long-term security while not only providing an income stream but also providing equity and long term income and wealth protection _NOT_ provided with most jobs.

Business ownership does come with risks. However, one of the most difficult things for many to understand is that it is often virtually impossible to eliminate risk unless one also eliminates opportunity. For many approaching or passing the age of 45 the risk of business ownership may be less than the risk of job insecurity, declining lengths of employment, declining pay scales and other factors.

Franchising in particular can often be an excellent way to reduce one's risk of business ownership by carefully evaluating the options available and using professionals, such as franchise brokers, accountants, franchise attorneys and other professionals trained in helping one evaluate the options. Successful entrepreneurs consistently have one thing in common - they partner with experts that have track records of experience. In life, one can learn from one's own trials and mistakes (which can be _VERY_ expensive) or learn through the trials, errors and expenses of others. Obviously, it is less expensive to learn from other's mistakes than one's own. Franchising by its nature allows one to use another's "recipe" and that recipe can often be evaluated through the investigation of the company's Federal Disclosure Documents and interviews with their current franchisees.

Finding a Better Version of You Through Franchising

One of the biggest challenges facing business ownership has been obtaining the funding necessary to start one's own business. The finance community has numerous options. We discuss funding in a later chapter.

Conclusion

The perception of control over a job, income and job security diminishes for many as one grows older. As skills, types of jobs and industries continue to change job security will most likely continue to be difficult to maintain unless one owns a business. Technology, ageism and worldwide competition are often accelerating those trends. One cannot expect an employer to have loyalty to their employees over their own survival and interests.

To best control of one's job security - find the right business. Become the guy that creates the job, which means becoming the employer versus the employee.

Why a Franchise Instead of Starting an Independent Business?

I am often asked "Why should I buy into a franchise system. Why not just start up an independent business?" It is an entrepreneur's world today. Here are five reasons you may want to consider becoming a franchisee of a business model that is already working as opposed to going it alone.

Brand awareness

If you walk into any of the 40,000-plus Subways or McDonald's around the world you are guaranteed your meal will be the same (or nearly) no matter where you are. That's the franchise proposition of uniformity and replicability. Customers know this and seek out the reliability and familiarity of their favorite brands, which have been established over years or decades.

Operating system

Entrepreneurs of independent businesses have to figure everything out by themselves.

Why a Franchise Instead of Starting an Independent Business?

A franchise allows you to skip the mundane and expensive pre-startup tasks and allows you to go straight to the exciting business startup. It still takes an enormous amount of work and resources but the franchise blueprint helps owners avoid the time-suck and financial mistakes that happen with a new concept.

Would you rather invent the wheel, or buy one ready-made? A franchised business provides a complete, out-of-the-box business, ready to "plug and play." Just follow the operating manual.

Equipment and supplies

Outfitting your new business with everything you need to succeed means researching what equipment to buy, finding suppliers, and negotiating deals. You may buy a pizza oven that's too big or buy more fresh food than you need; or you may buy one that's too small and run short on capacity as your business grows, or run short on pepperoni on a busy evening or weekend. Franchisors provide invaluable help in knowing both what and how much to buy, often at reduced prices.

Economies of scale

If you are a sole entrepreneur, you have the buying power of one. If you are a franchisee, your franchisor negotiates bulk rates with vendors based on hundreds or thousands of franchisees purchases and passes along the savings to you. Also, having the power of a recognized brand behind you often eases the mind of a supplier in extending credit: if a successful franchisor is willing to trust you, vendors are more likely to do so as well.

Legal disclosure

Franchisors are required by law to disclose certain information about their business in documents regulated by federal and state law. If you are looking to buy an existing business from an individual, can you (and your attorney) trust the seller? And if the seller disappears, where's your recourse?

Financing

Most new businesses require startup capital. While most franchisors do not supply financing, many have relationships with lenders who will view that brand's referrals more favorably than an independent business owner just starting out.

Marketing

If you are Joe's Pizza, you are on your own when it comes to marketing and advertising. If you are a Pizza Hut franchisee, you have the power of the brand's multi-million-dollar national and regional marketing and advertising behind you. If you are Joe, every penny to market and advertise your business comes directly out of your bottom line. Do you have the marketing skills and time to devote to this?

Speed to market

There are documented procedures and standards already in place to follow to help ensure your success instead of you creating your own.

You will receive pre-opening as well as ongoing support from the franchisor who shares information they as well as franchisees have learned that can help make you more successful and ensure your success.

You can build the most beautiful retail store or buy the perfect van for your mobile business and fill both with the most expensive equipment. That takes time as well as money. Or you can sign up with a franchisor who's done this hundreds of times and be handed a shopping list of exactly what you need to set up shop, allowing you to open for business more quickly than if you had to research it all on your own.

Why a Franchise Instead of Starting an Independent Business?

Faster ROI

No matter how grand your opening is, when you start your own business it takes time to build a client base and local reputation. When you advertise a known brand name in your new market, customers come ready-made and the cash starts flowing faster.

Training

You may be the best at what you do, but do you know how to manage a business, hire and train employees, market your product or service, keep the books, etc.? When you start your own business, you must learn all these things on your own, with "rookie mistakes" part of the learning curve. Franchisors provide new franchisees with extensive training in every aspect of their new business, from operating the business to which point-of-sale system to buy. And many offer advanced training to help you stay on top of your business as it grows.

Franchisor support

If you start your own business from the ground up, it is just you. Being a franchisee gives you the ability to be in business for yourself but not by yourself. You are trained and receive ongoing support on an established business model and plan and a proven operating system from the franchisor instead of figuring it all out yourself.

Most entrepreneurs (franchised or not) love what they do. However, caught up in the day-to-day details of such "mundane" details as marketing, advertising, taxes and purchasing supplies, they fail to innovate and to develop as leaders and executives. Many franchisors provide field support specialists who will visit your office every month or quarter to help keep their franchisees stay on track, training them to become managers and leaders "working on the business, not in it."

Finding a Better Version of You Through Franchising

Peer support

You are bigger and better as a team with others just like you. There is more power and recognition of a brand that is supported by many franchisees with many stores vs one non-franchised store run by a single owner. Subway was not successful with just one store, but only after they had several did they become successful.

Franchisees benefit from all the hard work, research, and trial-and-error that the franchisors and franchisees before them so the new franchisees entering the system can be set up for success.

As a franchisee, you receive ongoing support not only from your franchisor but also from your fellow franchisees. This support can come from locally, regionally, or at annual national conventions, through an online support network, or just by picking up the phone. Local business groups are invaluable for the networking connections they can provide, but who better to ask for help with your business than someone who's already solved the problems that you are facing for the first time?

It is like a family. You have a network of peers (fellow franchisees) all working together to help and support each other. You are a member of the franchisee family.

Franchisees communicate with each other creating a team-oriented atmosphere. Starting your own business from scratch can be a lonely experience with many feeling they are on an island by themselves. By providing open channels of communication, franchisees feel part of something much bigger and have the support network to succeed and thrive.

Product and service innovation

If you own a traditional business, it is your time and money that needs to be spent in order to test new products or services for your clients. If this new product or service proves to be unsuccessful it is your time and money wasted. Franchisors develop new products and try them in their company-owned stores or with other franchisees willing to test them. By the time McDonald's introduced its new line of coffees, the kinks had already been worked out. So while it may cost a franchisee some money to install new equipment or introduce a new store design, the ROI is more likely than with your own new great idea as an independent business owner.

Site selection

There is a lot of competition for lease space out there. Setting up your business on the wrong side of the street can severely hurt sales. You can hire a site selection expert, but what do they know about your business? A franchisor can provide teams of real estate experts, advanced site selection software, and years of experience in finding the best sites for their brand. They also can provide expert assistance negotiating leases with landlords, an often ignored and yet critical component of profitability.

Franchising offers a better chance to succeed

The U.S. Department of Commerce and other authors of statistics concerning franchising have shown that taking into account the indirect impact of franchised businesses; franchises support more than 13.2 million jobs, $1.6 trillion in economic output for the U.S. economy and 7.4% of the Gross Domestic Product (GDP).

Government research over the years has indicated that the success rate for franchise-owned endeavors is significantly better than the rate for non-franchise-owned small businesses. In short, the good news is that franchising makes up a significant part of the national economy and presents a statistically better chance for success than other business options.

The freedom factor

Most individuals seek three common elements when choosing a franchised business:

- Flexibility
- Money
- Status

These three elements are important for a variety of reasons and seem to be common denominators when people seek a new business as a career path. *Flexibility* has always been a hot button for entrepreneurs who exchange the stability of a job for the freedom that comes with being their own boss. *Money*, or income, is always a factor but surprisingly is seldom the most important. Many people have left huge salaries behind because they were miserable, to pursue the American Dream and launch a business. *Status* is an all-encompassing category that includes not only titles and position, but more importantly, the feeling of purpose one has and being a part of something significant in their own community.

Owning a franchise can provide you with all three of these elements if you operate the business successfully and manage your time and resources properly.

Happy franchise owners make more money

It is been said that if you love what you do, you cannot help but succeed. There is a lot of truth to this statement. If you can align yourself with a franchise that really fits, you'll be much happier, which in turn results in higher productivity.

Exit strategy/resale value

Selling an independent business can be very lucrative — but the pool of potential buyers is smaller than with a known brand. When faced with a choice between Carl's Jr. and Fred's Burger Boat, prospective

Why a Franchise Instead of Starting an Independent Business?

business owners often opt for the safety and familiarity of a known brand over a private business, just as consumers do when looking for a burger. And in tough times if you need to sell you may have to do so at a bargain basement price — if you can find a buyer at all. With a franchise there are always two additional buyers: the franchisor, which can always buy your unit and run it as a company store until they find a suitable buyer and many times your nearby fellow franchisees are looking to purchase other franchisees' businesses as part of their expansion plan.

Franchise Terms

The franchising industry, like all industries, has its own lingo. It is important that you become familiar with these terms as you speak with me, your franchise broker or a franchise development director.

Franchise disclosure document (FDD): All franchisors are required by the U.S. Federal Trade Commission to provide this legal document to prospective franchisees. FDDs are updated annually and consist of 23 sections, called items, which explain the company history, the fees and costs, contractual obligations, unit data and much more. Do not make a move without reviewing it. I have included a sample copy of a Table of Contents for an FDD in an earlier chapter.

Franchise agreement: The written contract, a copy will be included in the FDD, which outlines the responsibilities of both the franchisor and the franchisee.

Franchise attorney: There are approximately 1 million attorneys in the United States, and a couple thousand of them have chosen to specialize in franchising. Franchise attorneys know what to focus on in the FDD and in the actual franchise contract. They've probably written a few FDDs, so they know exactly what to look for when they're reviewing them for prospective franchisees. They also keep up on ever-changing franchise laws, including some that may be specific to your state.

Franchise fee: The initial fee paid to a franchisor to become a franchisee, outlined in Item 5 of the FDD. For some franchises this is a flat, one-size-fits-all fee; for others it varies based on territory size or other factors. Most franchisors offer franchise fee discounts for veterans, minorities, or for purchasing multiple units.

Franchisee: An individual who purchases the right to operate a business under the franchisor's name and system.

Franchisor: The parent company that allows individuals to start and run a business using its trademarks, products and processes for a fee.

Royalty fee: Franchisors require franchisees to pay a fee on a regular basis (weekly or monthly). Usually, it is a percentage of sales; sometimes it is a flat fee. Most franchisors also require a separate National Ad fee to cover franchisees' advertising costs.

Startup cost/initial investment: The total amount required to open the franchise, outlined in Item 7 of the FDD. This includes the franchise fee, along with other startup expenses such as travel expenses to training, insurance, real estate, equipment, supplies, business licenses and working capital for you to hit break even and start making an income.

Term of agreement: This spells out the length of time that your franchise agreement is valid--usually anywhere from five to 20 years. At the end of your term franchisors will allow you to renew your agreement for a small percentage of the then-current franchise fee. For a contract to be valid in the USA, it must have a beginning date as well as an ending date. At the end of your term the franchisor will send you a current franchise agreement for you to sign so you can continue as a franchisee. You do not pay the franchise fee again, but some franchisors may charge $500 - $2,000 to cover their legal fees.

<u>Units:</u> Synonymous with territories, stores or locations

Common Ways to Get Into Franchising

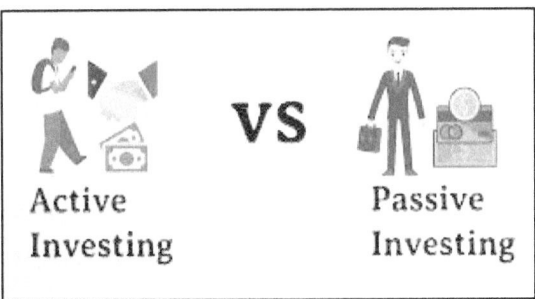

The franchising industry offers models for everyone. Some people are looking for a franchise to replace a job while other people are looking for an investment source – a business for them to invest in without having day-to-day operations responsibility.

Active ownership: The owner is involved in the day-to-day operation of the franchise. He/she may hire a manager to run the operations, a sales manager to run the sales side, etc. This is the owner's primary income.

Semi-passive ownership: An option offered by some franchisors allowing franchise ownership without being actively involved in the day-to-day operations. They hired a General Manager or Chief Operating Officer to run the business while maintaining their current career or enjoying retirement.

Many of my clients who purchase a semi-passive franchise do so for one of three reasons:

Common Ways to Get Into Franchising

1. They are hedging their bets. If they get laid off or restructured one more time they have a very profitable franchise to go into.
2. They are looking for an investment platform that will give a very handsome return.
3. They are either retired or close to retirement and want a retirement business.

Types of Franchises

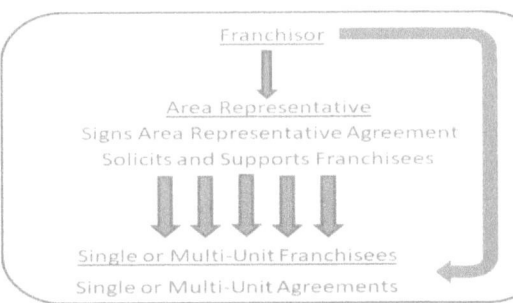

There are many ways to become a franchisee - single franchise, multiple units, area development and regional development. The lower in this list, the more expensive the option, but the higher the returns and wealth.

Single unit franchise: The lowest cost of entry. More direct contact with clients and employees. You purchase one territory and open one office.

Multiple units: More expensive but much more income and profit potential. Management based. You own two, three or many more territories. If service based you can run all territories with one office - one General Manager or Chief Operating Officer and one set of office staff. This offers multiple times revenues and profits but maintaining the same operating expenses as the single territory owner above. Franchisors typically give deep discounts for purchasing multiple units.

Types of Franchises

Area development: Develop units in an entire region, such as a city or small state. You and the franchisor will agree on how many units you would open every year. Managed by an area manager who manages managers. This area manager reports to you. This puts you as the CEO of a much larger business as the ones above.

Area representative or master franchise: This is a special type of franchise agreement that gives you the exclusive right to sell or open a given number of franchises in a large geographical area. It is common for Area Representatives or Master Franchisees to encompass large areas or areas such as large states or multiple states containing millions of people. You sell and support franchisees in your area. In return, you receive a percentage (usually 50%) of all franchise fees and royalties for the life of your business. Much more expensive but a true wealth model as you share franchise fees and royalties with the franchisor. This platform, although creating the wealth and lifestyle of a franchisor without having to spend the capital and time to actually become a franchisor, takes much more time to develop.

Maximizing Investors' Returns Through Franchising. Is Multi Unit, Multi Brand Ownership the Future of Franchising?

Since the 1940s, franchising has served as a vehicle through which small businesses have grown into successful national chains. Franchises have a high success rate, making it the business model with the lowest failure rate. As such, franchising is a thriving strategy through which individuals and small businesses can grow and prosper.

In the beginning - First wave

Franchising has undergone a fantastic evolution in the last few decades. The present-day franchised business now attracts a variety of investors for a variety of different reasons. Beginning in the early years of the 1960s owning a single unit franchise was an entry point for everyday individuals to get into business. This "First Wave" in franchising was the growth tool of choice for many entrepreneurs and first-time business owners.

Maximizing Investors' Returns Through Franchising. Is Multi Unit, Multi Brand Ownership the Future of Franchising?

With success comes change – Second wave

Many of these successful individual franchisees seeking growth went on to open numerous locations under the same franchised brand name. Using their experience in operations and developing staff as well as their ability to leverage cash flow from their profitable businesses, many went on to open additional units in the '80s and '90s. Whether it is a single individual owning three to five franchised units or larger investors that opened scores of locations, multi-unit ownership proved to be a method for financial growth by giving franchisees and investors an established model with a predictable result. Using this Multi-Unit development method as a means to increase enterprise value for the business owner became what I call the "Second Wave" in franchising. Many of these now professionally managed "corporate" franchisees have taken numerous franchise systems to new heights by developing scores of units in their designated territories.

All dressed up and nowhere to grow – Third wave

So what happens when a growth-driven franchisee reaches a level of saturation for their brand in their market? How can they continue to expand? How do they optimize the business infrastructure they've already created in their organizations? Or how does the institutional investor – investment groups and Private Equity firms invest in franchising?

Today's "Third Wave" of franchise development lies in the concept of not only owning multiple units of the same brand but also owning multiple units of various brands. Multi-Brand franchising has exploded in recent years. Countless franchisees now operate two, three or more non-competing brands in the same vertical market. These large franchisees can sometimes develop additional brands in their original territory while many others choose to run units in several regions. These franchisees are driven by revenue growth, brand diversification, open territory, capitalizing on existing human resources, consumer trends and demographics in a market. The concept of owning multiple units of one brand has been eclipsed by what is now known as Multi Brand ownership. That's where a franchisee develops the business enterprise as a franchisee of various non-competing brands.

Private equity investors dig deeper for gold

Today, not only are the franchisor/parent companies the target of private equity investment and acquisition but so are large franchisee organizations. As franchisees, private equity firms are creating millions of dollars in profit by scaling the number of franchised units in their portfolios utilizing a proven system with a predictable result.

Phil Druce, Partner with Atlantic Street Capital says "We feel strongly about the sustainability of the franchising category as multi-unit franchisee investors into the future. While some equity investors might shy away from broadly defined retail thinking that the category over the medium to long-term will be compromised with the proliferation of technology or delivery-based solution, we continue to feel positive about the sector."

Druce continued; "Amazon risk will continue to be a popular phrase used across the industry as an undefinable risk. We feel as though the best operators and investors will find ways to engage with the customer in a meaningful way, and deliver a customer experience that keeps people coming back. The most sustainable businesses will complement their core business with technology solutions of their own that enhance, without cannibalizing, their value proposition."

Investment groups large and small look primarily for four things when investing in a company:

1. Sustainability
2. Scalability

Maximizing Investors' Returns Through Franchising. Is Multi Unit, Multi Brand Ownership the Future of Franchising?

3. Short term and long term ROI
4. Controlling their local market

Of course these groups are interested in other quantifiable aspects to the business such as management, capital needed, place in the market and the market itself, etc. Many of these groups are now looking at franchising. Franchising can be a low-risk investment when done right. Private-equity groups are buying franchisees that control markets, which enable them to control local marketing and avoid losing reputation from the poorly-run mom-and-pop businesses down the street.

In the last ten years these groups have become more interested in becoming an area developer with multi-brand franchises systems. A good franchised system will fly out to the new franchisee's territory and help them find their COO who will be responsible for all daily activities, leaving the group to become the CEO of their new business. The COO reports to the managing partner of the group and the board itself. In the case of multi-brands the group may wish to have the franchisor help them find a COO for each brand.

So what is an area developer with multi-brand franchises systems?

The area developer: An area developer is a franchisee who agrees to purchase and develop a very large area in the form of multi-units being developed over an agreed upon time schedule. This area may be a large city or a small state. Many of these investment groups are interested in owning the brand in their entire market. Perhaps that is the Seattle, WA MSA (Metropolitan Statistical Area - a term for a combination of an entire area surrounding the city); perhaps it is the Houston, TX MSA. Working with the franchise development director we may learn that the area of interest may have 10 – 40 franchised territories to be developed. The group negotiates to purchase all those territories under a development schedule. The terms may be that the group agrees to purchase all 10-40 territories upfront and will open

2,5, or 7 territories (whatever agreed upon with both parties) every 12 – 18 months until all are developed. With service businesses you may be able to open all territories with just one large office or office/warehouse, keeping your operating expenses down.

The multi-brand system: A multi-brand system is a system usually owned by a large franchise group. This franchise group typically own 5 – 20 other franchised brands all in the same vertical markets. Because I am most attracted to service franchises (lower startup costs, faster startup and ROI, and much higher returns than food or retail franchises) a good example of buying multi-brands in the same vertical would be purchasing the rights to develop the entire MSA for a maid franchise, a lawn care franchise, a window care franchise, and a house painting franchise. Now the group owns the exclusive rights to develop these four franchises in their MSA and they can run all four out of one large office/warehouse in order to share expenses. This keeps revenues high, operating costs low and because these four businesses have different busy seasons the overall business never has a downturn. This business, once developed may hit top end revenues of $20MM - $30MM, with 20% - 25% net profits. When the group is ready to divest its holding, this business may sell for 5-6 times EBIDTA.

In the above examples the group may decide to purchase and develop the rights to just one of the franchised brands and concentrate on that one service/product. Other groups may want to develop two or more of the brands to diversify their holdings in a local market.

I have seen groups come in and purchase the development rights to all of Denver, CO MSA for three franchises all owned by the same parent group and all in the same vertical market. I've also seen a group do the very same thing in purchasing the development rights to all of South Florida for the same three franchised systems.

&

Can You Build Wealth With an Area Developer Franchise Opportunity?

Is your objective to build wealth? Do any of the following statements apply to you and your search for a franchised business?

- You have leadership experience, i.e., guiding others either in your job, business, school, church, civic groups, sports teams, volunteer groups, or other organized settings.
- You have business and/or financial management experience
- You are seeking a larger-than-normal business opportunity that will generate notable income and respectable equity over a 2-5 year period.
- You can commit to an investment of at least $100,000 that is obtained through either your existing resources, investment partners, or a lending institution. You do not need a passion for the end product. The business itself can be your passion.
- You have the vision and the willingness to build a business throughout a fairly substantial market, e.g., a metropolitan area, one or more counties, part of/whole state, multiple states, etc. (NOTE: Different franchisors offer different sized territories.)

Can You Build Wealth With an Area Developer Franchise Opportunity?

If you said yes to three or more of these you might want to consider building a multi-unit franchise operation. Typically these businesses enable an individual (or family/company/group of investors) to generate a legacy income and build more equity. They also require larger investments than do single-unit franchises. And they are more difficult to obtain. The franchisor is very discerning when it comes to awarding this type of opportunity. When the match is right, however, the rewards are also notably larger. Family dynasties can be built with multi-unit franchise agreements.

NOTE: My wife and I owned and built a multi-unit franchise operation for several years, and we loved it. It was a very rewarding experience to build it...as well as to sell it. If you decide to investigate this type of franchise opportunity in your area, I will be happy to relate our experiences to you.

Types of multi-unit franchise offerings

Please allow me to briefly outline the different types of multi-unit franchise structures that many U.S.-based franchise companies use today.

Area development agreements

Typically this type of franchise offering simply allows a person/company/group to build and own more than one unit franchise within a defined geographical area.

Most often, these agreements are "single tier" arrangements, meaning that the holder of the multi-unit agreement agrees to build all of the unit franchises in the designated territory themselves (no "sub franchising" to others) and the parent company agrees to provide all of the support to the franchisee (no middle entity between the parent company and the unit franchisee).

These agreements almost always contain a negotiated development schedule, in which the franchisee agrees to open "X" number of unit franchises over "Y" months or years. The number of units can vary according to the arrangement between the franchisor and the franchisee. Most companies have pre-determined criteria for determining how many unit operations can be built in a designated territory. Often the initial franchise fees are discounted after the initial unit.

Restaurant franchise companies commonly use single-level area development agreements to build their brand throughout a McDonalds sign designated area. McDonalds used this mechanism in their "early days" to create those "McDonalds Millionaires" that you have heard about for years.

Regional franchise agreements

Regional franchise agreements are "two-tier" arrangements, in which the parent company authorizes the regional franchisee, often called a regional director, to do two things:

1) Recruit qualified individuals to own the unit franchise, and

2) Provide local support to the unit franchisees.

In exchange for these two business-building functions, the parent company financially rewards the regional franchisee the following income sources for the life of your business:

1. Paying the regional director a portion (typically 50%) of the initial franchise fee ("the franchise fee") for each unit franchise they award in their designated region.
2. Paying the regional director a portion (typically 50%) of the on-going royalties paid by the unit franchisees throughout the lifetime of their franchise agreement.

Can You Build Wealth With an Area Developer Franchise Opportunity?

3. Some companies who sell products to their franchisees also include some type of bonus commission to the regional director, based on wholesale purchases made by the unit franchisees in the regional territory.

In essence, regional director is awarded the right to build the respective business over a defined geographical area. They are compensated for doing so and the regional director has the right to sell the business. The relationship is defined by a 2-way agreement between the parent company and the regional director.

Several franchise companies use this form of multi-unit franchising to create more rapid growth of their business throughout a large geographical area, such as a county, a state, or a section of a country. For example, Century 21 used this mechanism to dominate the residential real estate market in the 1970s and 1980s. Most recently, Orange Theory Fitness and Massage Envy have used this approach. These companies success in doing so is legendary.

Master Franchise Agreements

Master franchise agreements are USUALLY the same as - or quite similar to - regional franchise agreements. This term is often used to refer to countrywide agreements for a country (or part of a country) outside the USA, e.g., Mexico, England, Spain, etc. Some franchisors use this designation inside the U.S. also.

Clarifying Notes

Different companies can use these terms in different ways, so you ALWAYS need to be sure exactly what a specific company means when they use one of these three terms. Two franchisors can use the same term to refer to two different multi-unit business formats.

For example, the term area development agreement can be used as a generic term to apply to any or all of the arrangements outlined above. The terms "master franchise" and "regional franchise" can be used interchangeably to refer to the same business arrangement.

My thoughts on multi-unit franchise agreements

I am reasonably well versed in multi-unit franchise arrangements. As noted above, my wife and I built a very large multi-unit franchise. In addition I have placed candidates in multi-unit franchises throughout the U.S.

Not all franchisors issue multi-unit franchise agreements, while others prefer to do so over issuing single-unit agreements. Some franchisors will do single-tier area development agreements, but will not do two-tier regional franchise agreements. Other franchisors will do all three types of arrangements, e.g., single-unit agreements, area development agreements (single-tier), and regional franchise agreements (two-tier).

To take their business to an overseas country, the vast majority of U.S. franchise companies prefer the master franchise agreement so the parent company has only one entity to work within each country. Otherwise, international expansion can get a bit cumbersome.

Conclusion

All companies are reasonably "picky" when evaluating a potential candidate for a multi-unit franchise agreement. They want to make sure the person/company/group/family they select has the financial resources, business experience, and personal characteristics necessary to build their larger businesses.

Sometimes it makes sense to consider this form of franchising and other times it does not. When it does make sense and a person's qualifications are in order, and the opportunity fits all the parameters then the multi-unit and area development franchise models can provide the franchisee very high returns and an enviable lifestyle.

Can You Build Wealth With an Area Developer Franchise Opportunity?

Remember: For multi-unit franchise offerings, companies are NOT seeking experts in the "end-use" of their products and/or services. Instead, they are looking for individuals who have the desire, skills, resources, and support to build LARGER multiple-area businesses. Typically they are looking for individuals who can lead people and manage money and time. These are "executive-style" business opportunities.

If you have big goals and objectives for the business that you build, being an Area Developer or Master Franchise owner may be the route for you. We can discuss the possibilities.

Funding Options

4 Funding Options to Raise Startup Capital for Your Business

Financing is crucial in getting your business up and running. You need to ensure you have the working capital necessary to sustain your business from startup to break even.

As your franchise broker I have relationships with many leading franchise funding companies. These companies offer a wide variety of financial services, such as 401(k) rollover, unsecured loans, and Small Business Administration assistance.

Funding sources available

Personal savings: Before you make a big withdrawal I recommend that you have at least a 6-12 months of fixed living expenses (like your mortgage and insurance needs) set aside or have a spouse/partner to cover your living expenses as you grow to break even.

Funding Options

When you are starting your own shop, you may have to forgo a salary for a few months up to a year, before you gain traction and income starts flowing.

Retirement plan rollover: Did you know that you have the ability to use your retirement fund(s) to invest in your business without penalty, interest or tax due and debt free from the IRS? An innovative program developed by the IRS in 2004 allows people to use their retirement funds tax, penalty, interest and debt free for all business startup expenses. The Rollover Business Startup plan is governed by the IRS and the DOL and has been legal since the Employee Retirement Income Security Act (ERISA) of 1974. The short and long term benefits of this program has now resulted in this becoming even more popular than SBA loans for funding franchises. This proven funding source will allow for your business to start debt-free and cash rich. It is not a debt because it is not a loan. The IRS looks at funding your business under this platform as just another investment from your current retirement funds. Instead of investing your retirement funds in mutual funds you are investing in your business.

Even if you still need to get an SBA loan, you can use the proceeds from your retirement fund rollover as your down payment. These funds can be used for any business expenses – franchise fee, working capital, salaries for you and family members, company car (which you also depreciate), etc.

The SBA offers several plans for the new franchise owner. Below are two of the more popular:

SBA Express Loan - $50k - $150k
- SBA working capital loans ranging from $50k - $150k.
- Not collateralized.
- The loan term - 7 year with a 25% down payment and interest rate of Wall Street Journal Prime Rate plus 2.75%.
- No pre-payment penalty.

- Off the books – does not affect credit ratings.
- Can take 2 – 4 weeks.

SBA The Dream Loan - $150,000 to $350,000

- SBA working capital loans ranging from $1500, 000 to $350,000.
- The loan term - 10 year with a 25% down payment and interest rate of Wall Street Journal Prime Rate plus 2.75%.
- No pre-payment penalty.
- Collateralized with business assets, however, personal assets may be required to be pledged as collateral if needed.
- Can take 2 – 3 months.

In addition **the SBA offers**:

- **The SBA 7A Loan** from $350,000 up to $5,000,000.
- **Equipment Leasing** from $10,000 up to $500,000.

SBA loan requirements

- Required Credit Score must be 675 or greater.
- Minimum equity injection as well as the required reserves needed per SBA Guidelines range from 10% - 30% of the requested loan amount from non-borrowed sources (checking, savings, cash withdrawal from retirement/Rollover, stocks and bonds).
- Bankruptcies must be released within the past 5 years, no open judgements and/or tax liens.
- Evidence of US Citizenship or proof of permanent residency.
- Cannot generate a loan approval without the signed SBA documents.
- Once Approved, Dream Loans are expected to close within 30-45 business days.

HELOC stands for <u>H</u>ome <u>E</u>quity <u>L</u>ine <u>O</u>f <u>C</u>redit, or simply "Home Equity Line". It is a loan set up as a line of credit for some maximum draw, rather than for a fixed dollar amount. Most HELOCs are second mortgages. An increasing number, however, are first mortgages, as yours would be if you used it to refinance your existing first mortgage.

Conclusion: Our funding specialists can discuss this with you further in detail with no obligations on your part. They can even pre-approve you for all loans or retirement rollovers for free. This way you can find your financial reach before you spend too much time reviewing franchises. Like purchasing a house, you need to see how much you are pre-approved for before house hunting. The same principle applies with purchasing a franchise.

Franchise Due Diligence

Franchise Buying Process

Grand Opening
Training
Agreement Signing
Attorney Review
Meeting Team
Due Diligence
Brand Discussions
Initial Conversation

My well-designed research process efforts for my clients provide much more information about a franchise system than can be acquired on the internet or talking directly to the franchise development director. He will tell you what he wants you to know. I will find out everything you need to know.

I am an expert in helping people find the best franchise for them while avoiding many costly business search mistakes. Also I am independent of all franchising systems; therefore I am not biased towards any of them. My goal as your franchise broker is to provide you the information that you need to determine if franchising is even your best option, doing a market study in your area to help determine which products or services are not being served well in your area, researching the best franchises based on your unique business skills as well as your financial and lifestyle goals and help locate funding options you may not be aware of that can save you thousands of dollars. Once we define your skill sets and business/lifestyle goals I will perform research on your behalf to create a professional presentation on three or four franchise systems you may want to learn more about. And best of all, I am free to you, the franchise candidate, as the franchisors pay me out of their marketing budget. Just think of me as your free franchise consultant.

You may be surprised that the process of purchasing a franchise normally takes two to three months. After you and I have one or two calls to better define your business skills, industries you are most attracted to and financial/lifestyle goals we will make an appointment to go over a market study I will generate for you. On this call we will also review more about what franchising is all about. And we will go over in detail your funding options, some of which you may not even be aware.

At this point I will do a complete franchise research on your behalf, followed by a presentation of the research findings. During this call I will present a professional PowerPoint presentation showing 3-4 franchises you may want to learn more about (based on everything I have learned about your background, skills, goals, etc.). You will learn about their history, how many franchisees they currently have, their franchisees earnings claim, total startup expenses for the franchisee to hit break even and so much more. You will probably have interest in learning more about these franchises. I will schedule an introductory phone call with you and the franchise development director for each of these franchises. I will be on all calls and I will moderate those calls on your behalf. Remember, you are learning, not buying. You are never under any obligation. Everyone I introduce you to understands this and understands too that their job is not to sell, but inform. During weekly calls with the franchise development director you will learn much information about their brand. You will speak with their active franchisees. These franchisees are doing the business every day. This is your opportunity to see what their thoughts are on the system (for example, are they happy? Did the franchisor provide good training? Are they available for support? Is the franchisor proactive in their support? How much money are they making?) You'll also speak with the franchisor's support team and their CEO or President to talk about their focus for the future.

The franchisor will at one point ask you to fly out to join them to get to know everyone at the home office and tour one of their local branches. This is called the Discovery day. This is your day. You will be introduced to your support team and the executives. Here is your opportunity to ask the executives about any future developments. You may also tour one of their local branches.

As we go through the process together you will begin to discount the franchises we are talking with, one by one, as not being the right one. You and I will discuss this and as your franchise broker I will contact the franchise director and tell them that we have gone in another direction. Towards the end of the process you normally will have just one franchise that you are excited about. Once you come back home from Discovery Day (and not one minute before) is the time to make the "Yes" or "No" determination. If "Yes" then the franchisor will send over a franchise agreement, you will sign it and send it back along with your franchise fee. Next, pack your bags for training.

I have a typical franchise due diligence process and timeline for your review on the next page.

Franchise Due Diligence

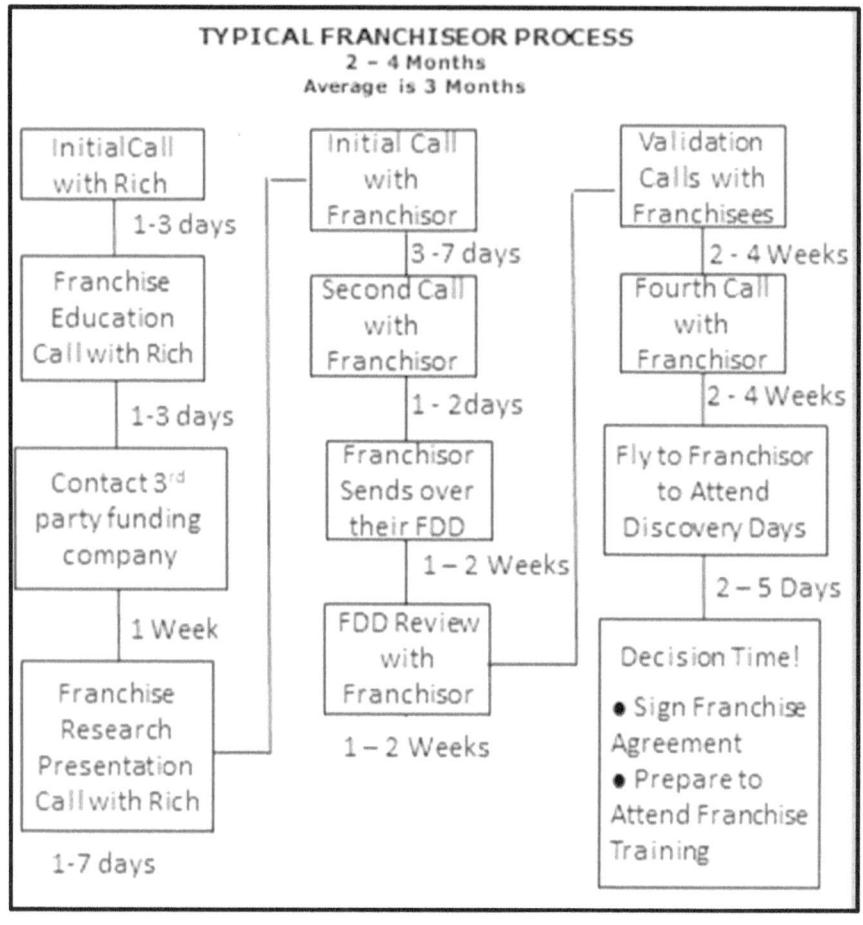

TYPICAL FRANCHISEOR PROCESS
2 – 4 Months
Average is 3 Months

Initial Call with Rich	Initial Call with Franchisor	Validation Calls with Franchisees
1-3 days	3 -7 days	2 - 4 Weeks
Franchise Education Call with Rich	Second Call with Franchisor	Fourth Call with Franchisor
1-3 days	1 - 2days	2 - 4 Weeks
Contact 3rd party funding company	Franchisor Sends over their FDD	Fly to Franchisor to Attend Discovery Days
1 Week	1 – 2 Weeks	2 – 5 Days
Franchise Research Presentation Call with Rich	FDD Review with Franchisor	Decision Time! • Sign Franchise Agreement • Prepare to Attend Franchise Training
1-7 days	1 – 2 Weeks	

Why Do I Pay A Franchise Fee?

Franchising is a strategy that the franchisor uses to achieve its objectives, including market penetration and market domination. Franchises are granted or awarded to a qualifying franchise candidate that has similar objectives in their own marketplace. That franchisee will have the responsibility to fully implement the operating and marketing systems of the franchisor in their defined area for a specified period of time.

The franchise fee is not necessarily a profit stream for the franchisor. It is the cost of putting the franchisee into the business of the franchisor. Costs include:

- The development costs of all of the elements of the Franchisor's system.
- Training the Franchisee to use those system elements and programs.
- Creation of franchisee's website, then initial Search Engine Optimization and Search Engine Marketing.
- Marketing and advertising to find candidates.

Why Do I Pay a Franchise Fee?

- Costs of qualifying candidates including rejecting many unqualified candidates.
- Salaries, travel, & administration.
- Legal expenses to draft agreements defining the methods & terms for the franchisee to participate, etc.

It is the franchisor's responsibility to cover those costs. In other words, the franchise fee is the entry fee from pre-training to the franchisee's grand opening.

To the franchisee it must represent a reasonable fee to allow you to become a part of the existing system, including all of the training programs that are a part of that system, to help you reach your own business goals.

Why Do I Pay A Royalty Fee?

 The first point to make about royalties is that good franchise systems should look at them not as a payment but rather as a remittance. It is the franchisor's share of the income derived from customers or clients. The franchisee collects that fee along with all other revenues from the customer. The royalty fees are built into your pricing structure that your franchisor will help you set.

It is an important concept because it emphasizes that the customer ultimately pays for everything, including the franchisor's royalty, the franchisee's overhead, all costs of sales, employee's salaries, and the franchisee's profit. Therefore it is all about the customer - as it should be.

The franchisee should want the franchisor to earn a reasonable amount of royalties because that's really the oil that makes the engine run. Each franchisee collects and remits a small portion of that oil to the franchisor. All elements of the system can continue to improve as long as the royalty stream is strong.

The franchisor's royalty will be based on the fact that they have provided a system and strategy that has ultimately served the customer. The franchisee delivers that system to that customer. The royalty represents the franchisor's share based on the various parts of the franchise system, which has four elements.

The four elements of a franchise are:

1. Brand
2. Operating system
3. Support system
4. Franchisee

Brand - The name associated with the services delivered in a memorable and satisfying experience to the customer.

Operating system - Institutionalizes the excellent service delivered in a memorable experience so it can be done over and over again from franchise to franchise in a consistent manner.

Support system - Helps the franchisee get better and better at delivering the service in a memorable experience - helps a franchisee improve their performance.

Franchisee - The individual motives or reasons for being in a good system, as well as the talents and experience delivered to the business.

The operating and support systems will generally provide access to advice at the level of professional consultants in the fields of marketing, management, advertising, execution of the delivery of the product or service, customer support, etc. The cost of these types of consultants on the open market will often far exceed the value of the royalty fees that are remitted by the franchisee that participates in a system that delivers these items from a position of experience. In fact, it is the exact experience the franchisee requires as opposed to open market advice

Now here's the test. If each of the four elements of a franchise system is evaluated in terms of the percentage of contribution to the overall success of the business, then the royalty can be assessed in a proper light. Many people will say that each of the four elements contributes equally - or 25%, to the overall success. That means that the Brand, Operating system, and Support system provide 75% of the success formula. You, the franchisee provide the remaining 25%. Therefore, as long as the royalty is less than 75%, it is a good decision to participate in the system. That's a little silly as most royalties range from 2% to 10% depending on the type of system.

Keep in mind that your royalty also pays for testing and developing new products and services for you, their franchisee, to offer to your customers. Without the franchisor spending the money to hire the consultants and employees to keep up with newest product, service and marketing trends your business will soon get stale. Imagine McDonalds without its breakfast menu.

Your royalties also pay for the franchisor to continually monitor the franchisee's website in order to maintain high rankings on the search engines.

Franchisor's Qualification Process

One of the initial things you should strive to understand is the level of development that the franchisor's candidate qualification process has reached. Your first reaction to that might be "Why do I care about a franchise qualification process? I only care if I get a franchise or not." I would suggest that you should care a great deal.

After all, if the franchise candidate qualification process has not been well developed, it may be a reflection on the business of the franchise itself. The most important asset of any franchise system will be its people, including both franchisees, and franchisor staff. Almost all franchisors will confirm that to be the case.

If people are the most important asset, it would follow that the process of finding, approving, and granting franchises to the best franchisees would be a well thought out, and well-developed process. Does that make sense?

Franchisor's Qualification Process

If there is no formal step-by-step process to provide information to both parties then it may be an indicator that there is something amiss.

A good process will be able to provide you regular information to help you make an informed business decision about joining as a franchisee. It should also provide the franchisor with information about you to help them make an informed decision as well. That decision should be whether you qualify as someone they can describe as one on their "most important assets".

If the process does not allow for a step-by-step evaluation, a process of information flow to you and from you, then perhaps the other business systems within the franchise are also not as well developed as represented. The information process should not be so fast that you are overloaded, but it should be steady enough that you can continue to assess, and deliver information, at a pace that makes sense for both parties.

If the process is too fast I would suggest there is something wrong. To rush is to err. On the other hand, if the process is too slow, you will not get a true flavor for the company because of the sporadic nature of the information flow. Culture is important, and a steady flow of data will give you a better feel for the culture of the business than trading information every three weeks for a six-month period. If you are not looking to make a final determination within 30 to 120 days, I would suggest that you wait until you are at that point before you engage fully in a franchise due diligence. That does not mean that you need to be in business in that time frame. It just means that you would like to make a determination in that time frame.

Most information sharing processes will include a step-by-step process where you will receive information from the franchisor, and then you will be required to provide some information to them. Once you provide the information the franchisor will send you additional data to help you gain more intimate knowledge, and so on. The reason for that type of process, which I would judge to be ideal, is that each of you is illustrating commitment to the process. This is an important factor for the franchisor to determine because it is a great indicator to them that you will be able to follow and use a good process to your advantage. That's what franchising is all about. The franchisor has invested a significant amount of time and money to develop a proven process that is designed to earn all stakeholders a maximum return. Therefore the franchisor must determine that each new franchisee is willing and able to follow a good process. What better place to start than the basic evaluation process.

In today's world, that process should use various media to communicate with you including email, telephone, mail or courier, internet, in person etc. Again, this will demonstrate the franchisor's use of current technologies and methods to really get to know you, and to stay current in an ever-changing global environment.

How to Know When it is Time to Quit Your Corporate Job and Buy a Franchise

A lot of franchisees come from the corporate world. Frustrated with the rat race and tired of working for someone else's dream, they decide to make the jump into entrepreneurship. With so many success stories of people going from the boardroom to business ownership, it begs the question: How do you know when it is time to quit your corporate job and invest in a franchise?

1. You are passionate about entrepreneurship.

Ten percent of prospective franchisees in the USA are looking to open a franchise because they dislike their jobs. However, opening a business should not be done as a reaction to disliking your job. It is a lot of hard work and if you are not truly passionate about it, you could easily falter, even with the backing of a franchise. Going the franchise route does give you a head start in business ownership, but it is not like you can buy a franchise and then put it on autopilot to run itself. If you are frustrated with your job then business ownership might be a way out, but do not let job frustration be your only reason for wanting to open a franchise. Passion about business ownership should be your key motivating factor.

2. You want to build up your own equity.

The problem with working in a corporate position is that no matter how good your job is, and no matter how much you enjoy it, you are working for someone else's dream and you are building someone else's equity. When you retire, you may end up with a handsome pension but you will have worked for decades to make money and equity for the business owner or the investors.

When you own your own business all the profit you make is yours and you own something that you can be proud of and that you can sell to set yourself up for early retirement. Or if you grow your business enough you can step away from the day-to-day running of it and invest in other businesses, building yourself a portfolio. When it is time to retire you cannot sell a job, but you can sell a business.

3. You love a brand and want to be a part of it.

There are different ways to become part of a brand. You can own stock in it, you can be a loyal customer or you can own a franchise location (providing the brand is a franchise, of course). If you really love a particular brand and that brand is a franchise, there is no better way to be a part of it than to own a location so you can carry on everything you love about the brand and represent it to customers.

4. You are able to fund a franchise location.

You cannot just decide to open a franchise location and then do it. You have to be able to procure the financing first. Do you have enough saved up and do you have enough equity to get a business loan? Many franchises will help you find the necessary funding to start a location, but you also have to be in a situation where you will be able to fund the franchise location you want. There are franchises in all investment levels, from just a few thousand dollars up to hundreds of thousands of dollars. We discussed funding in a prior chapter "Funding Options".

5. You are dissatisfied with your current situation.

As mentioned previously, investing in a franchise should never be a sole reaction to your current situation, but being dissatisfied with where your life is currently can be a major motivator for business ownership. If you find yourself constantly wishing to be your own boss and your job brings you no satisfaction, it might be time to consider entrepreneurship.

6. You do not want to always ask yourself: "What if?"

When you are retired and living out your twilight years, do you want to look back at your life and know that you lived it to its fullest potential? If you have any sort of inkling for entrepreneurship and you do not bother to ever explore that path, you are likely going to be asking yourself "What if?" when you are older. What if you went for it? What if you invested in a franchise when you were younger? Would your life have been better?

What Can I Do to Stop Being an Employee?

Stop Being an Employee &
Start Being a Boss!

It is not surprising that many who are unhappy with their situations have considered business ownership. Recessions come and go and have been known to encourage entrepreneurism and increase the number of small business start-ups. Entrepreneurial efforts in the U.S. are at a 14-year high. It is great for the economy and it is an excellent opportunity for the business owner.

The economy relies on new small businesses by providing jobs, services and products for consumers, and an increase in spending by other business owners. Entrepreneurship and small business growth are cornerstones to the increased growth of our economy as a whole. According to the SBA small businesses - defined as an independent business with fewer than 500 employees - employ half of the U.S.'s private sector employees and have generated 65% of net new jobs over the past seventeen years. There are more than 27million small businesses in this country, and they generate about 50 % of our GDP. Franchised businesses account for 7.4% of our nation's GDP.

Starting a business can replace lost or reduced income, replace an unhappy employment situation, or give the business owner flexibility in their work-life balance that they cannot experience in a role as an employee or provide an investment for their portfolio.

There are many benefits to starting a business and they are going to vary depending on your individual situation.

You choose your schedule, where you work, with whom you work and how many hours you work. Business owners choose their own schedule, they work when it is convenience for them (whether that is when the kids are in school, late at night, early in the morning, etc.). They have the flexibility to choose their own time off and how much time they can take off. They select whether they work from a home office (reducing the stress and cost of commuting) or from an out-of-home office location and they choose the style of office environment in which they want to work. They even choose all of the people with whom they work - employees, clients and vendors. They have the advantage of choosing to work with only people who help them achieve success. This has an immediately positive impact on the work-life balance of a business owner.

There is an old saying "Come on in, the water is fine". If entrepreneurism and franchise ownership is something you'd like to consider, my contact information is on the back cover. Contact me for an initial conversation. We'll discuss your financial and lifestyle goals and see how I may be of assistance. Remember, the process and focus is not about buying a franchise. It is all about learning more about franchising to determine if this is even the right option for you.

Franchising Makes Business Ownership Easy

Franchises work better than independent businesses for so many reasons. It is easier; you have a quicker break-even point and a lot less stress during the process. Some of the reasons that you break-even more quickly are based on the simple fact that franchisors have a ready-made operating and marketing , business and marketing plans, big-buying discounts and ongoing support.

As a franchisee you would join the group of sometimes hundreds of other businesses buying the same exact products as you, but who are not in competition with you. This allows you to get big corporation benefits on a small business budget. This decreases costs, which in turn increases profits. Producing a million dollars or more in sales, those savings add up quickly and are evident in your expanding bank account.

Franchising is a popular model because it provides a formula that has been proven to be successful multiple times before. After all, franchising is following a proven formula for success. Successful business people have recorded their systems and processes so that the method can be repeated - by you.

Franchising can increase your chance of business success by minimizing your risk through:

1. Proper planning: Information in the FDD gives exact expenses, allowing you to properly plan income needs and costs.

2. Support of the group: When operating a business within a franchise system, you not only have the support of the franchisor, you have the support of your fellow franchisees. You have the opportunity to learn from them, ask questions and discuss your options with people who have direct experience in your business.

3. Established operational systems: It takes an incredible amount of time to create and refine systems that help your business operate smoothly and successfully. A franchise has established and perfected these systems, so you can focus on the core activities of your business.

Franchising takes the guesswork out of starting a business and puts you on the fast track to success.

Be in Business for Yourself, but Not by Yourself

 GreatBusinessSchools.org recently published an infographic entitled "Foray into Franchising" which provides an incredibly helpful overview of franchising. Some of the key points are listed below.

The article shared some key percentages, such as 55% of franchise owners own multiple territories. The article also estimates that the franchise fee is typically around $30,000-$50,000, though it does vary greatly depending on the type of industry or even the franchisor itself.

Franchising is an exciting form of business ownership, but as with any endeavor, there are always pros and cons. The article recommends four questions to ask you:

1. **Your investment:** How much money do you have available to invest?
2. **Your abilities:** Does the franchise require special technical training or education? What skill set can you bring to the business?

3. **Your goals:** Do you intend to run the business yourself or hire a manager? How many hours are you able and willing to work a week?

4. **Your potential franchise:** Is there a demand for the franchise's services or products in your area? What's the level of competition on a local, regional and national level?

I can help you figure out if franchising is right for you and, if so, which concept best meets your needs and qualifications.

What Are the Keys to Franchise Success for Franchisees?

Making any business reach its full potential takes talent. If you've selected your franchise well, your franchisor will be able to help you avoid many of the mistakes new, independent start-up businesses make. Here are some keys for franchise success.

Make sure you have enough money

- Determine how much you have to invest and how much you will need to live on for at least 6-12 months.
- Make sure you understand the initial investment required.
- Make a careful and rational decision about buying the franchise. Listen to your franchise attorney and accountant.
- Speak with our 3rd party funding specialists. They can pre-approve you for free, giving you a very good idea how much you can obtain to finance a franchise.

What Are the Keys to Franchise Success for Franchisees?

Follow the system

- Franchisees sometimes get their business up and running and then begin to change, add or modify existing products, advertising, hours, services, and even the quality and consistency they are licensed to deliver. This violates the franchise agreement and puts them in jeopardy of having their franchise terminated!
- By following the system, you:
  - Preserve the brand.
  - Protect your investment and that of your fellow franchisees.
  - Will rise to your successes much faster – why spend the money to join a franchise then start changing the very systems and procedures you paid for?

Do not neglect your family and friends

- Be prepared to work long hours at first, but also make sure to budget time for your family and friends.
- Do not forget to acknowledge the sacrifices your family makes.
- Allow your family and friends to share in your new life.

Be an enthusiastic franchisee

- The success of any business is linked to the level of enthusiasm you bring.
- Enthusiasm brings a level of excitement and energy to the operation that everyone can feel - including your customers and staff.
- Let your staff in on the fun. Acknowledge their good work with recognition or a raise.

Recruit the best and treat them with respect

- Good help is hard to find - great help is essential.
- To keep the good staff you've hired:
    - Rotate routine and boring jobs.
    - Be fair. Do not show favoritism.
    - Work with your staff to develop the schedule.
    - Treat your employees with respect. Do not allow employees to be disrespectful to any other employee.
    - Keep employees informed of new marketing and other promotions.
    - Remove hassles - ask employees which procedures are working and which are not.
    - Make their workdays challenging.
    - Provide timely performance reviews and wage salary increases.

Teach your employees

- In franchising training should be continuous. Employees are your front line.
- Training classes are a good way to show your employees that they matter to you.
- Get all the training for your employees you can from the franchisor.
- Regularly train and retrain all your employees.
- Hold refresher and advanced classes on a regular basis.
- Alert your franchisor when you need additional training.
- Take advantage of every training opportunity, whether it is offered by the franchisor or by local schools, trade associations and other sources.

What Are the Keys to Franchise Success for Franchisees?

Give customers great service

- The most important thing you can do is to get everyone to smile.
- Let the customer know you are happy they chose your business.

Get involved with the community

- Customers like to shop in places that support their community.
  - Sponsor a Little League team.
  - Support a civic or youth group.
  - Give tours of your business for school groups.
  - Set up a kiosk at community events.

Stay in touch with your franchisor and other franchisees

- Stay in communication with the franchisor: Letters, newsletters, emails, phone calls, faxes, training classes, regional meetings, conferences and conventions.
- Communicate with other franchisees by participating in the franchise owners association. Meet local franchisees monthly or quarterly for lunch.
- Attend all national and regional meetings with your franchisor.

Watch the details

- Success is in the pennies! If you watch your pennies, the dollars will take care of themselves.
- Watch out for shrinkage (merchandise that is missing or unaccounted for).
- Work hard every day. Choose your time away from the franchise wisely. Enjoy life!

ॐ

What Goes into an Exceptional Franchise?

Today there are over 4,500 different brands operating over 850,000 franchised units in the United States. But why does franchising work, and how can it work exceptionally?

Proven operating model

Much of the risk and capital outlay for an independent business owner lies in developing, testing, and refining a business model. In a franchise, the franchisor has already accepted that risk, capital investment and responsibility. Everything from site selection to operating manuals, to technology platforms and marketing strategies and tools should allow a new franchise owner to hit the ground running.

Branding

Anyone who has raised children in the United States in the last 50 years can relate to this. You are driving down the road. Your kids are hungry. They see two signs ahead; one for McDonalds and the other for Bill's burgers. Where do you think the car is headed? We are a nation brought up and driven by brand and brand loyalty. Your ability to capture market share and capture it quicker largely depends on the brand and brand reputation that your franchisor has established.

Network of owners

As a franchise owner, you are not alone. Not only do you have the corporate staff of the franchisor seeking to help you succeed, but also the dozens, hundreds or even thousands of other franchise owners who have "been there done that" and are usually eager to help new owners succeed as well.

These are some of the main reasons why the franchising accounts for about 7.4% of the GDP in the United States alone.

But how and why should franchising exceed extraordinarily?

Management team experience

The operating models, marketing, support strategies, etc. is driven by the senior management team of the franchisor. The ability and willingness of the franchisor to collaborate with franchise owners along with a "win-win" mentality is crucial to exceptional and long-term success for both parties. Look at the track record of the management team. Have they succeeded in building other franchise brands? Is there a high commitment and low turnover of personnel at the corporate level? What do the franchise owners say about the leadership team of the franchisor?

Partnership mentality

One of the keys to building long term, cohesive relationships between franchisor and franchisees is the approach that the leadership takes with its franchisees. Does the management team view the success of their franchisees as their main focus? Their mission? Do they view their franchise owners as partners building a brand? The most successful franchise brands now and in the past come to the understanding early on that if their franchisees do not succeed then the brand does not succeed.

Franchise owner selection

The best and most successful franchises typically are very selective on who they "let in" to their family. This comes full circle. If the franchisor is providing best in class support, tools, service and support to their franchise owners then the franchisor is expending a great deal of personnel and capital to do so. As such, it behooves them to make sure (as sure as they can) that they are only bringing in the best and brightest owners into their family. Anything short will result in incremental time, support, investment on the franchisor side, and possible failure/closure/resale on the franchisee side.

Your Road Map to Success

The old saying is there are only two guarantees in life - unfortunately, neither of them are "You are guaranteed to be successful." But, what if you had a roadmap that helped you determine a route to your best success in business?

Franchising is the system that can provide just that. Franchisors provide a franchisee's earnings claim in the Item 19 of FDD. The FDD also contains contact information for existing franchisees for you to validate the earnings claim information individually. The active franchisees already in the system can provide you with a great deal of information on the system and what's needed for success.

While it is true few things in life are guaranteed, preparation and education can come close in making you feel just as secure.

Quiz: Ten Signs that You are Ready to be Super Successful

The more you know about yourself, the more able you are to make the types of changes required for real success and growth.

How insightful are you about yourself? Are you curious about knowing the inner workings of your psychology? The more you know about yourself, the better prepared you are to make the types of changes required for real success and growth.

According to David Dunning, a social psychologist at Cornell University, "There are many reasons why it is hard to know ourselves. In a subjective area like intelligence, for example, people tend to perceive their competence in self-serving ways. A student talented in math, for instance, may emphasize math and analytical skills in her definition of intelligence, while a student gifted in other areas might highlight verbal ability or creativity."

Quiz: Ten Signs that You are Ready to be Super Successful

Obtaining feedback can be helpful, Dunning says, but we often disregard critical feedback by nature. And people are prone to overestimate themselves out of ignorance: Take the ironic example of an elderly man who thinks he's an excellent driver but is a hazard on the road, or the person who reads a book about the stock market and is ready to compete with a professional stockbroker.

The bottom line? It is hard to know for sure if we are as knowledgeable of ourselves as we may think we are. So here are 10 statements to help you access your insightfulness about your career and life. Answer yes or no and tally the number of times you say yes.

1. I know my greatest strength and purpose and use them to navigate my career.
2. I am aware of my psychological baggage and understand the repetitive patterns I create for myself in relationships and in my career.
3. I am aware of the negative self-talk I create in my mind and how different that is from reality.
4. I know why I have failed and can identify lessons I have learned from each of those failures.
5. I am often more curious than decisive.
6. I do not succumb to fearful thoughts often because I feel confident in my ability to work with fear and face it when necessary to conquer key goals.
7. I ask for feedback from my colleagues, partners, and friends, and I do not get defensive when I hear critical statements they may share.
8. I enjoy pushing my comfort zone and proactively. I seek opportunities that are part of my future vision but also scare me, in a good way.
9. I am a good listener, and in conversations end up doing more listening and asking more questions than talking.

10. I am open to having support to help me take my career, my relationships, or my personal awareness to another level.

If you answered yes:

> **8-10 times**: You are not only self-aware, but you are also curious, thoughtful, and have a growth mindset. Being open to change, being collaborative, and working well with others are all considered superstar qualities from some top companies. Continue to strive to be your best self and, honestly, the sky's the limit.

> **4-7 times:** You are on the path to self-awareness and being insightful about your strengths and weaknesses and how you engage with others. You may have just started thinking about how you impact others and what that impact is. It could be that you have recently had a life event that has prompted some deeper understanding of yourself. You may be contemplating a big career change and need a plan of action. Either way, you are on the right track. The more aware you are of yourself, the more positive your career and life will be. You may consider asking your colleagues, partners, or friends for some pointed feedback on how they perceive your impact. This could be a powerful step toward getting more self-insight and having a bigger impact on others.

> **0-3 times**: You have little, if any, insight into yourself, your potential, or how others experience you. It may be time to think about the value you would gain by knowing yourself more and the influence that is possible when others feel seen and heard by you. You may not be open to getting support, but it could mean no longer running up against the same challenges and having less-than-satisfying relationships. Getting support now could be a game changer for you: a life

you love, instead of one spent feeling like there could be something more.

Owning a Franchise Business Can be a Great Second-Act Career Move

The last kid is off to college on a new exciting adventure and the house is very quiet. Now that you can hear yourself think, what _do_ you think?

It is been a long time since you had a new adventure.

Your job is no longer exciting or challenging.

You are not excited about retirement that's just around the corner.

You still dream of owning a business and being your own boss.

If facing an empty nest has you reevaluating your life, maybe it is time to dust off some old dreams and see if they still fit. Moving on to a second-act career could open up a whole new world of possibilities by channeling your hard-won expertise into something completely different, moving to a new place for a fresh start, finding time to do things you love that fell by the wayside, or focusing on giving back to your local community. With a career that you control instead of it controlling you, like owning a franchise business, there are options.

Owning a Franchise Business Can be a Great Second-Act Career Move

We at Nations Franchise Source are dedicated to helping people fulfill their dreams through franchise ownership. The business models of the over 400 brands in our portfolio position my clients, the franchise candidates, to be as successful as they want to be with a robust infrastructure of training, support and networking. Each franchise candidate can choose the form their business will take, including number of territories, full or part-time, manage a crew or crews, or do the jobs themselves. Over the past 12 months more than 20 new franchise owners have come onboard with my help as their franchise broker and their reasons for a second act may resonate with you.

Need something new in life

- She and husband looking for something else to do.
- He quit a job of 20 years to start new.
- Now retired, but bored.
- Good fit for his personality and interests, leaving a 30-year job.

Want to own a business

- Wants to run his own business and work with his wife.
- She was a stay at home mom for 16 years but now that her youngest is in school she got bored and wanted to start her own business.
- Wants to create and leave to their children a legacy of wealth.

Better work/life balance

- He was working so much his wife said he needed to find a different job.
- Burned out, always wanted her own business; will allow them to have more time together.
- Works nights, married 13 years with three small children; wants better hours and family time, not working night.

- Wife works over 80 hours a week and wanted to start a business together to spend more time together; they want to build a future.

Job security and retirement

- Been downsized three times in last five years, got a new job and was laid off again.
- Wants to work for himself and have more control.
- This will be their retirement plan. Own it for 10 to 12 years and then sell it.
- Wants better future, looking to retirement, has a passion for organization and helping people.

A second-act career does not always mean nearing retirement, but it definitely means taking steps to change your future, and on your own terms.

Five Signs that You are Standing in Your Own Way to Success

While a lot of the entrepreneurs I've met and mentored in the past decade have been successful, I've also met some unsuccessful entrepreneurs. Each of them seemed to make a lot of the same mistakes -- ones that could be easily remedied, but when left unaddressed, could mean the difference between success and failure.

Here are five signs you are getting in your own way to success and how to move over and let yourself be the best you can be:

1. You are unable to complete a task before starting a new one.

Some entrepreneurs just cannot finish. For whatever reason, it does not matter how much time they have or how many resources are available to them, they cannot focus and get something done. Maybe it is the fear that their final product could be better, or they're worried it is not perfect and they will not be able to make changes later.

But Seth Godin got it right in his book "Linchpin: Are You Indispensable?" when he wrote: "The only purpose of starting is to finish, and while the projects we do are never really finished, they must ship. If you miss deadlines and are always late, in the end, you'll have little to show for yourself".

I always say, if it is ninety percent there, it is good enough. Because: you must ship. Perfect is the enemy of good.

2. You micro-manage everything.

Unsuccessful entrepreneurs want to do everything themselves. They do not believe anyone else can get a job done as well as they can. But even if they were actually right about this - which is doubtful since no one is the best at everything - it is an unsustainable business philosophy.

If you want to grow your business and become a leader, you are going to have to learn to train and trust others. Everyone needs a support team -- even the most competent people.

3. You are always right.

I've noticed that it is difficult for some entrepreneurs to admit when they've made a mistake. But if you fail to acknowledge a mistake, you miss out on a learning opportunity. Mistakes are stepping-stones to success. Ask for advice and admit when you are wrong so you can quickly move forward and do better.

4. You ask questions, but do not really pay attention to the answers.

You know the type of person I'm talking about. They ask for your opinion, but they're only really interested in what you have to say if it is exactly what they already believe. That baffles me. These kinds of entrepreneurs surround themselves with people who will only ever agree with them. That's bad for business. You'll make better decisions if you abandon your stubbornness, truly weigh different points of view and try to understand other perspectives.

5. You always find reasons not to move forward.

The timing is not right. The economy is not doing well. The economy is doing too well and must be nearing a downturn. You do not have enough capital. Whatever the excuse, you always have one. But guess what? There will always be reasons to not move forward! You just have to decide to press on. Create options for yourself, be flexible and have courage. That's really what it is: having the courage to take on risk.

As entrepreneurs, we all make mistakes. That's part of the fun of being willing to take risks. But over the years I've learned that the more humble and receptive you are, the more likely you'll succeed.

Seven Questions that You Should Ask Yourself When Faced With a Tough Decision in Life

 When you are faced with a tough decision in life, you may feel paralyzed and at a loss as to what is best to do. When you are stressed, or trying to deal with a dilemma you may question your own rationale, and worry that your final decision may not be wise.

There are certain questions you can ask yourself when making a difficult decision to find out if your reasoning is good, and if you have found a wise solution to your problem.

Here are seven of the best questions I have found to guide you when you have to make a tough decision.

1. If I do not do this now, will I regret it?

It is sensible to consider the long-term implications of any decisions you make, because you do not want to end up doing something you will regret in the future. But it is equally important to consider what might happen if you do not do something. If you do not want to end up in a divorce then never get married. If you do not want disobedient and disrespectful children then do not have children. But look at all those great memories you would have missed if you had let the fear of regret set in. Do not let important opportunities pass you by because they involve making some big decisions. Ask yourself what you may gain, or lose, in the long-term by making certain choices.

2. What am I afraid of?

People often get stuck with decisions because they are scared of what will happen if they make a choice. Some people are afraid of failure, but others are scared of success. Ask yourself whether fear is going to make this decision, or are you when facing a tough decision in life.

Are you making decisions based on facts or emotions?

3. What does my gut say?

Often times we take too much time to make a decision because we're afraid of what's going to happen. As a result of this we go through things like careful planning, deep analysis, and pros and cons before deciding. We are waiting for that sign to appear (by the way, which never occurred in any other major decision you had to make). Instead, learn to trust your gut instinct. For the most part, your first instinct is usually the one that is correct or the one that you truly wanted to go with. I always say "Do not listen to your heart. Do not listen to your head. But _DO_ listen to your gut". Going with your gut makes you a more confident decision maker compared to someone who takes forever to decide.

4. Why am I really doing this?

The wisest decisions you can make are those that keep the end in mind. If your end goal is a better lifestyle for you and your family, a better work/life balance, or more freedom in your life then making the big decision to start a business, for example, might be a step closer to that. Have your goals clearly in mind when making big decisions.

5. Who am I really doing this for?

Do not let others' agendas or advice sway you from making the right decision. It is always important to have others' interests at heart when making a decision, but you should not always sacrifice your own needs and desires to please another person. Take a balanced look at how your choices will benefit you as well as others when facing a tough decision in life.

6. Will I like myself after this decision?

Anyone can make a difficult decision that ticks all the boxes in terms of a solution without taking into account how that decision may make them feel about themselves. If you make a decision that is callous or uncaring you might not end up liking yourself very much. If you make one that is unassertive your self-esteem is likely to drop. Consider how you will feel about yourself for making this choice whenever you have to make a tough decision in life.

7. Are you just postponing your decision until…later?

Many times after my client has gone through the entire due diligence -they have all the information they could possibly need to make their determination – They have spoken with very happy active franchisees – They have visited the home office to speak with their support team and the executives.

They know and agree with the executives' focus for the future. They tell me "Rich, let me think about it for a while." It is normal to need a few days, maybe up to a week to think it over. However, you just spent three months gathering data and talking to the franchisees. You have everything that has ever been printed or spoken about this system.

I understand what is going on. They are letting the fear enter into their psyche. All of a sudden, it has gotten "Real". I think that subconsciously they are hoping that the clouds will part, the sun will shine a beam on their faces and the angels will sing as a sign. But unfortunately that just is not going to happen.

This is the time my client needs to go back and read my chapter on fear, and about listening to your gut. If you find yourself postponing any big decision until "Later", ask yourself – "What will be different later than now? Is this just postponing the decision?" The decision still has to be made. And remember, if you do not make the decision, the decision has been made and that decision is "No". If you do not act one way or another, then the event does not happen so by default, the answer is "No". As an example, do you remember back years ago in more youthful times wanting to ask someone out. You really wanted to go out with this person but you were afraid they would say "No" so you did not ask them. You were afraid of rejection. So in effect, you made the decision without making a decision. You decided "No".

Beware the Ambush!!

Making the transition from the corporate world to business ownership is a big enough transition by itself without listening to everybody else's opinion on the subject. And yet, guaranteed, you are going to hear a lot of other people's opinions on your new venture (or possible venture). That's normal! And it is normal for you to want to hear what other people have to say about it too! But there are some pitfalls to be aware of along the way that are so common that numerous articles have been written about it.

One of the largest "clubs" on earth is the "naysayers club". No matter what the idea is, it is an easy task to find the naysayers to squelch the flames of passion and progress. Whether it is a spouse or family member, a friend that "knows about these things", a business person "experienced" in these matters, an advisor that is looking out for your best interests (translate that to - do not advise clients to take any chances because I might get blamed), or someone else, there will always be a multitude of people to tell you why you should not do something.

That's not to say that the advice of people close to you, and people you respect, should not be obtained and considered. It should. However, it should also be considered as only a part of the formula and not the primary decision criteria. If naysayers had the final say, we would still be in the dark ages because all progressive ideas, all leaps of faith that have driven our progress and our dreams over time would have been fire hosed by the naysayers' clubs of the past. They are everywhere and always have been. They say things like "pull in the reins", "batten down the hatches", and "dig in your heels".

I have a note on my monitor I see every day that says, "Do not get caught in the negative norm". The reason the note is there is because it takes a conscious effort to look at things in a positive light because our natural response to things is a "resistance response". That can lead to erroneous judgments based only on the negative. It is just the way we're engineered, and as long as you are aware of that natural human inclination to the negative, you can weigh those responses accordingly and make a proper evaluation of opportunities.

Of most importance is inner self-doubt that cements us in place. We think things like, "it will never work", or "who am I to do that. The result of those types of thoughts is self-defeat.

Those successful people we all aspire to be think much differently than that. They think, "I'd rather confront the challenge. I am good enough to succeed. I'd rather *"just do it"*!"

Everyone has a choice on how they approach life, and the opportunities that are presented to them, either with gusto or timidity. Let the naysayers rule and timidity will never be defeated. Consider the naysayers' opinion - just make sure they are not simply

"Business Prevention Specialists" - and approach opportunity with gusto and the world will open up.

Dreams are achieved only with gusto.

How to Get Past the Fear of Buying a Franchise

Fear can have an incredibly negative effect on franchise candidates. It can prevent you from making the right decisions, stop you from taking calculated risks, and have profound effects on your attitude and mindset. In business, a small amount of fear is healthy. However, too much fear is likely to hold you back. Here we take a look at different ways franchise candidates can help themselves overcome the fear of failure.

First, let me say that the fear you are experiencing is perfectly normal – every one of my clients has experienced it at one level or another. I know I did when I purchased my first franchise. After all, fear prevented our caveman ancestors from playing with T-Rex, right? It is perfectly normal to have feelings of fear when you are thinking about buying a franchise. Fear is a good protector, but fear can also prevent us from accomplishing important goals because we mistake risk as fear. Let's see if I can help alleviate some of these fears for you.

How to Get Past the Fear of Buying a Franchise

You may be experiencing one or more of these fears

Transition fears

You may be worried about the transition you'll be making if you decide to move forward with the franchise opportunity you are interested in. The transition I'm referring to is from employee to employer. And it is a big one. The reason it is so big is because of all the new responsibilities you'll have as the owner of a franchise. You'll be responsible for things like:

- Hiring
- Payroll
- Inventory
- Marketing
- Operations
- Business Development
- Expenses

And part of your fear has to do with the fact that you may not know how to do all of those things.

The good news is that when you are a franchisee, you'll receive formal training on every aspect of your franchise business. It is part of what you are paying for. In essence, by the time you are done with training, you'll have the knowledge and the confidence you need to run your franchise business. The franchisor will be there as you open your doors, holding your hand and "Showing you the ropes". As a result, your transition from employee to employer will be much smoother, and less scary. Remember the joke "How do you eat an elephant"? The answer of course is "One bite at a time". All these tasks will come at you one at a time and the franchisor is there all the way with you.

Finding a Better Version of You Through Franchising

Financial fears

Investments can be risky. That includes an investment in a franchise business.

That's why it is important to:

A. Make sure you can afford the franchises you are investigating by building projections showing cash needed until you hit break even. The franchisor will help you with your projections by giving you a projections template for you to use in making your own projections. You'll talk with as many of their franchisees as you'd like to learn from them what incomes and expenses you should be projecting.

B. Choose and research the franchises you are interested in carefully and methodically. This is where I can help you the best.

Doing those two things can help you lower your risk. The best way to walk through your fear is by doing everything you can to minimize your financial risk, like doing great research and staying within your budget.

Fear of failure

This fear tends to rear its ugly head right when you are about to make your "yes" or "no" determination on the franchise opportunity you've been investigating. But do not kid yourself; this fear has been a part of your psyche ever since you had your first call with franchise headquarters. It just finally got "Real".

There are specific things you can do to ensure you are making a good, well thought out decision. Here they are:

1. Take the time to learn everything you can about franchising.
2. Make a commitment to only look at franchises you can afford.

3. Only look at franchises that offer an opportunity for you to use your top skills.
4. Do good research. That includes talking to 10 or more active franchisees already in the system. See how they overcame their fear of failure.
5. Write a thorough and realistic business plan.
6. Hire an experienced franchise attorney who will look out for your best interests.
7. Do not allow yourself to be rushed into anything.
8. Make sure those closest to you are on board.

Here are steps to help you overcome your fear or anxiety

Step back and consider the long game

Much of the fear we experience and the pressure we place upon ourselves is unnecessary. We do it to ourselves. A lot of it originates from the short-term attitude of many franchise candidates. Rather than stepping back and considering the long game, we often consider the fear of a small setback to constitute an enormous problem.

Do not be overly Self-Critical

While a certain amount of self-criticism is necessary as a franchise candidate (a franchise candidate who considers themselves perfect is likely to be deluding themselves), too much criticism is not healthy. Opening a franchise is the biggest challenge most individuals will face in their professional careers. It can be testing and trying at the best of times. It is made even more difficult if you are constantly at war with yourself and overly self-critical.

In one sense, too much self-criticism is simply counter-productive. Typically, those with an overly negative attitude spend more time pointing out what's wrong with something than do working out how to work through it. This prevents individuals from moving past certain problems and means they're doomed to repeat their mistakes.

Finding a Better Version of You Through Franchising

Being too self-critical can also have a big impact on your general outlook, mindset, and attitude. Run yourself down too much and you'll soon find that any positivity is gone and self-doubt reigns supreme.

Surround yourself with Good People

Good franchisees surround themselves with good people. An intelligent franchisee understands that they're not going to be able to handle every issue on their own and that they're going to need some help and support.

Advisors come in many shapes and forms. They can be friends, colleagues, mentors, associates, or you can pay for their services. Whatever their status, it is important that you trust them and respect their opinion. Advisors can help you through tricky times by offering a second perspective, emotional support, or suggesting a route through your current problems. In some cases, it is just important to have someone there to talk to.

Franchisees often find that their fears are reduced by the simple act of expression. Just talking about your problems can help relieve much of the tension and calm your nerves. There's a reason that most successful businesspeople develop strong support networks around themselves – they act as both a pressure valve for fear and nerves, as well as being a source of good advice.

Adopt the Logical Mindset

Fear is an emotional response. Sometimes there's a logical basis for your fear, but not always. Franchise candidates can often overcome their fears by taking a step back and analyzing that fear, their circumstances, and the determination-making processes they are currently involved in.

Adopting the logical mindset is what we do in most complex situations. With any question, such as whether a particular franchise investment is safe or whether you should trust a certain franchisor, the only way we can improve our chances of reaching the right answer is by arming ourselves with all the relevant facts. Generally, the greater our rational understanding of something, the less fear we feel towards it. Step back and think "Is this what I think, or is this what I know"? Is it a perception? Or a misperception? If it is what you think, let's get you the information you need so it is what you know.

Conclusion

As I've said previously, some fear is only natural. However, a strong fear of failure is likely to prevent you from reaching your full potential. Franchise candidates need to develop ways of managing fear as best they can if they're to truly investigate running a successful business. While it can be scary to become your own boss, using the suggestions I included in this chapter will go a long way in lessening your fears, and may increase your chances of success.

As you can imagine, the most powerful, the most successful people have faced the fear, acted upon it, and realized that they can push through it. That realization is a tremendous springboard to prosperity. Susan Jeffers, a noted Psychologist and Author said "_**Feel the fear and do it anyway**_".

Compare where you are now in your career with where you were with your first job. Chances are you just left college. You only knew what your college professors told you. You just jumped into your new career. You were not expected to have the same knowledge and skills as someone in your career for 15 – 20 years. And you knew that from the beginning. Your learning did not stop after college. You adjusted to the new challenges in your career. In a way, this is what you are doing in franchising. Do not tell yourself that you cannot possibly be successful because you do not know anything about this business. You will get trained (just like in college, but with the focus of one subject, not several and no football games to attend. No kegger parties this time around.) And like your corporate career, you will be surrounded by a very knowledgeable and helpful support staff.

If I had to summarize six steps or thoughts to deal with the fear of failure they would be:

1. Act boldly.
2. Persist and never, ever give up.
3. It is not personal.
4. Change things, change results; keep things the same, do not expect different results.
5. Ease up on yourself - tomorrow is coming anyway.

Look for possibilities - there are always alternatives

One final thought about this subject - **fear incapacitates unsuccessful people**.

It is Not the Right Time

"As soon as the mortgage is paid."

"As soon as the kids are done with college."

"As soon as I get my buyout at work."

"As soon as I learn everything there is to know about it."

"As soon as I am absolutely sure that this venture will have zero risk and my astounding success is guaranteed."

Again, these thoughts are absolutely paralyzing. They are very real thoughts, and most are perfectly legitimate thoughts, but only thoughts and not reality. However, as I said, they are paralyzing.

There is a quote by German writer Goethe that has always intrigued me and it seems to strike at the very heart of this issue. *"There is one elementary truth the ignorance of which kills countless splendid plans: that the moment one definitely commits oneself, and then providence moves too. All sorts of things occur to help one that would never otherwise have occurred. A whole stream of events issue from the decision, raising in one's favor all manner of unforeseen incidents and meetings and material assistance which no man could have dreamed would come his way. Whatever you can do, or dream you can, begin it. Boldness has genius and magic in it. Begin it now."*

In my companies we had a saying, and it was long before Nike made it famous as their advertising slogan. Whenever, anyone hesitated to tackle a project, or to take a risk, or to take that next step to get the job done, we would simply say, "Just Do It"! My title in my businesses was simple and direct. I was the CMIH - Chief Make It Happen.

That attitude does not suit everyone, but then perhaps it should. My guess is that it does suit those successful people we dream to be. The point is that the time to act is very likely now, when the opportunity is present, as opposed to some ill-defined "when...then I will..." Stated another way by Author Marsha Sinetar, *"Intentions count as nothing if we do not translate them into action".*

How Do You Know If a Franchise is Right For You?

Franchises are complicated yet simple. The best ones have spent years fine-tuning their processes; their systems, their brand and their marketing so that their franchisees can step in, follow the script and prosper.

This is the best-case scenario.

Unfortunately, what sometimes happens is that franchisors sell themselves this way but do not always have the infrastructure, systems or processes with which to back it up. These are the franchises you must avoid. Just because the franchise business you are interested in does something that appears to make money, always remember that that is just one part of the equation of what you are actually purchasing. The bigger question is - do they have the system and the follow through and the infrastructure to make your business life easier. After all, that is really what you are paying for. So, how do you know if a franchise is right for you?

How Do You Know if a Franchise is Right For You?

Below are seven things to consider before you decide on a franchise.

1. Have you met with a franchise broker, franchise attorney and accountant?
2. Do you have a clear understanding of the business model you are buying?
3. Do you know where you thrive?
4. Do you have a handle on the money and other revenue sources?
5. Do you want to buy one or many?
6. Have you spoken to other franchisees and former franchisees?
7. Do you want to be actively involved with the day-to-day activities or be semi-passive?

There are undoubtedly other things that you must do before you buy a franchise. But these seven things will certainly help you along the way. Always remember that buying a franchise is the start of a marathon.

I Want to Buy a Franchise. So What's Next?

One day or day one.
You decide.

Unknown

Realizing that you want to buy a franchise is the first step on a new, exciting path. But if you've ever searched the internet for anything, you know there is a ton of information out there and it is not always easy to organize or understand. Google the term "Franchise" and you'll receive 588,000,000 results. Do not waste your time slogging through countless websites that do not really have all the information you need.

This is where I come in! I am an experienced franchise broker who has over 30 years' experience in franchising as a franchisee in two separate systems and as a franchise broker having gone through intensive training to complete my Certificated Franchise Broker and my Certified Franchise Consultant certifications. I can help you every step of the way.

What kind of franchise model would work best for you? What industry? Home-based or brick-and-mortar? What can you afford?

I Want to Buy a Franchise. So What's Next?

What are your financial and lifestyle goals? What fits your personality and business skills? Do you want your weekends and evenings free? Will you be an active, managing day-to-day activities franchisee or a semi-passive franchisee hiring a COO to manage day-to-day activities? These are just some of the many, many questions I can help you answer.

How do I do this? I have many tools at my disposal that are designed to help you get the answers to these, and many more questions you may have along the way. Just one of these tools is my business builder profile assessment. This science-based, market validated and franchise specific profiling system is way more than just some personality test. In fact, it is not a personality test at all. Instead it is a scientific meta-analysis approach that indicates your values, stages of growth of the franchise you'd be most successful in, the culture you would most enjoy, comparing your work style to that of the franchisor's franchisees, your business skills, your sales style, the perfect business path for you and your emotional and social intelligence assessments.

All of these areas, and more, will play a huge role in determining your future success. You do not want to start a new business on the wrong foot. Let me help you figure out exactly which type of franchise system is most compatible with you. I believe anyone can be a successful business owner if they discover the right opportunity. My contact information is on the last page of this book. Please feel free to reach out to me for more information.

Ten Reasons to Use a Franchise Broker

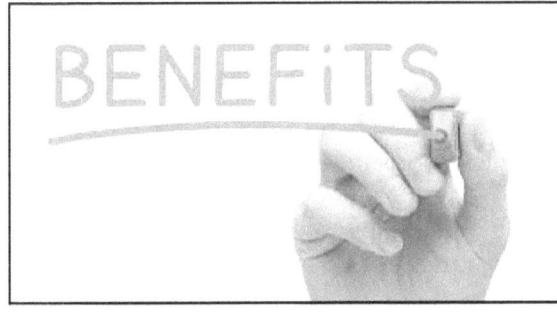

For most people, starting a business is a once in a lifetime event. It is essential to utilize available resources effectively and "get it right" the first time. A franchise broker uses an established process that helps match a person's talents and goals with the right franchise which ensures a much higher success rate. As your franchise broker I act as your strategic advisor throughout the process to be certain you are making a selection based on facts and not speculation. My goal is to educate my clients about the many different businesses without having to go it alone. My services are free so there is no need to go it alone! Remember, we will be working together not to buy a franchise, but to learn if franchising is even the right option for you. And there is never any obligation on your part.

When it comes to buying a house, we call a real estate broker or agent to guide us through the journey and to help us to ultimately make the right purchase. Our attorneys counsel us on our legal matters. We have financial planners to help us determine our best investments. In

Ten Reasons to Use a Franchise Broker s to Use a Franchise Broker

franchising most potential buyers rely on franchise brokers like me and here are reasons why.

1. I am an educator. With over 30 years in franchising, as both a franchisee and a franchise broker, I can teach you some of the things I have learned about franchising including trends, financing, and the realities of franchise ownership. I will answer your questions about franchising and guide you through the selection, ultimately helping you to discover if an opportunity makes sense for you.

2. You'll receive a market study for your area showing how your particular area will receive a new business. We will review the market study and look over the growth areas and what products and services your market needs.

3. We will go over funding options that you may not be aware of for financing a franchise. I'll introduce you to 3rd party funding specialists who will help guide you through your funding options. They even offer a free pre-approval so you are aware of your financial reach should you decide to purchase a franchise. Funding can take anywhere from two weeks to three months, so getting pre-approved early is to your advantage.

4. You'll receive a short presentation about franchising - what is this whole franchising thing all about? You'll learn much more working with me.

5. You need a good listener – that's me! By listening to my clients' needs and expectations, I can keep your interests in mind at all times.

6. Reducing your risk is my main goal and focus. There are always risks in any business, but with my 30 years' experience and background in franchising I can help you avoid many of the risks. I know what to look for, brands to avoid.

7. Once we get to that part of the process, I will moderate all calls with you and the franchisor. Learning about franchising and selecting the right franchise is a process of many phone calls between you and the franchisor. As a franchise candidate you will want to meet people who are already operating the business you are thinking about buying. You'll have the opportunity to speak with as many of their current franchisees as you like. We call this validation calls.

8. I will prepare you for a meeting with the franchisor. Almost every franchise company sponsors a Discovery Day which is an in-house information event. You will meet the executives of the system, your support staff, hear about the company's focus for the future and tour one of their local branches. I will help you prepare for the Discovery Day.

9. _All my services are free to you, my client._ The franchisor pays me out of their marketing budget - so franchise brokers do not take fees from their clients. Just think of me as your free franchise consultant.

10. *Each week you will receive a Free Copy of my weekly "Franchising Tips" email.* Each email will help you to understand what franchising is all about.

Please remember, you are never under any obligation to go forward and nobody - me nor any of the franchisors we will speak with - will ever try to sell you something. We all understand that our job is to get you information for you to make a qualified determination. This is all about learning, not buying.

Ten Reasons to Use a Franchise Broker s to Use a Franchise Broker

Working with a franchise broker, like working with a Realtor, can save you time, money and will lead you to the franchise that meets your expectations, budget and goals. And again, we are free to you!

By the way, people that I have worked with who have gone on to own one or more franchises have found it extremely fulfilling and a wonderful next step in their careers.

My contact information is on the last page of this book. Please feel free to reach out to me for more information.

How You Benefit from My Research

 Researching is not enough. You have to have the right research and know how to examine that research in order to make the best decision. As a franchise broker, I can help you do that. I spend a great deal of time researching for you. I weed through and examine hundreds of franchises to find the ones that are closest to your professional, financial and lifestyle goals. You benefit from this in several key ways:

Get prepared with the right questions

Just because you ask the franchisor questions does not mean they are the right questions. There are certain questions that must be asked in order to properly evaluate a franchise. I can provide you with some excellent questions.

Understand the terminology and processes

Franchisors use a different language. They have a whole set of terms not used in regular business environments. They also have specific guidelines and processes they must follow in order to be compliant with the FTC guidelines and their own industry practices. After all this is franchising, it is all about following a system and a good franchisor does exactly that. They follow the system that has been laid out and expect anyone interested in working with them to do the same. If you do not understand these guidelines and general processes it can be very confusing and frustrating. I can educate you on all of this, making your experience much more enjoyable and easy.

Introduce you to the right franchise advisors

As a franchise broker, I have access to some of the best franchise attorneys and CPAs in the franchise industry. Using a franchise broker allows you access to these professionals.

Epilogue

Thank you for reading my book "Finding the Best Version of You Through Franchising" After reading the book many of my clients went on and established the American Dream for themselves by contacting me and going through the process of learning more about franchising. Those who went forward with their dream of owning their own business have thriving businesses and could not be happier. Some of my clients decided that franchising is just not for them. We parted as friends and many I still stay in contact with. I thought that I should share my ending thoughts to you with a couple of personal stories.

My first story is about my biggest career regret. I graduated from my university in August 1978 with a degree in Computer Science. I came home from an on-campus interview with a company. My wife asked how the interview went. I told her "Very well. In fact they want to fly me to California to meet the founders". She asked if I was going to go I said "No, they want me to come on board as a marketing director and I want to be a programmer. Besides that, they have a stupid logo.

Epilogue

It is an apple with a bite taken out of it". You see, Apple Computers, as it was called then, had just stated up eighteen months before. Nobody had heard about them yet. So my first job out of college, I earned $10,200/year, bypassing the opportunity to do, well who knows what? Later on in life, once I finally realized the great opportunity I had and said "No" to I vowed to never say "No" to any other opportunity that came my way unless I researched the opportunity. I had just said "No" to an opportunity that, had I done the research, could have made me a multi-millionaire many times over. I would have been one of the first marketing directors hired by Apple. Think of the stock options I left on the table. Never say "No" to any opportunity until you have all the facts. Do not make these decisions based on opinions and emotions only.

My other story has to do with my wife's uncle. He died several years ago. I did not know him well, nor knew much about his story. He was my wife's father's brother. He had worked in an architecture firm in Dallas, TX. He owned a sailboat (and was more than willing to scare me on nearby lakes with it when we visited him). Before he passed he sent an email to his secondary family penned in a very matter of fact way. He was battling cancer and knew the end was near. His email simply outlined the finality of his life. There were very little happy memories.

The reality is people who are close to us will die. It is a part of life. But another part of life is, well, life itself. And, what should be a never-ending search for happiness.

It amazes me that no matter how many lives end (and many of them far too early) that people still struggle to find a happy place while on this earth. Sure, bad days happen, but as a new day begins we should always fight to find those happy moments. And, if you are not happy, you should change.

Finding a Better Version of You Through Franchising

We need to learn from those who came before us - all of those billions of people who have lived and died. Learn from their misfortunes and their blessings. But most of all learn from the fact that this life you live will go fast. You are not in control of the last breath, but you are in control of every other breath. Do not sit there not following your dreams. Do not sit there not believing in life. Do not sit there not believing in happiness.

No matter how many times we hear that life is short, we do not listen. You, me - all of us die. Too many of us think we are invincible. This is not necessarily a bad thing, as this mentality makes it easier to live through tough days. We as humans are given this great characteristic as children that should be maintained throughout one's entire life - hope. *__The hope and the will to live a great life__*.

Why do so many adults stop answering the questions of what do they want to be when they grow up? Why do so many of us not have bucket lists? Is not the drive to do what we want the ultimate meaning of life?

The beauty of franchising is that I can look at all of my clients and see hundreds of franchisees". They all followed their dreams by doing something that they wanted to do - own a business. I did the same two times.

Not everyone is cut out to be a business owner, though, but everyone is cut out to be happy and find the very "Best Version of You". If you work in an environment that does not make you happy - do something about it. Nearly everyone needs to work - why not be happy where you end up working? Change does not have to be quitting - change could happen by talking with your mentors/leaders and asking them how you get to a happier place.

Stop living the life you do not want to live. Start living the life you deserve. Even if the riches and fame you dream about seems impossible, start now - take steps toward whatever that happy place is. Do it with ambition, with your dreams wide open, and with no regrets. Without risk, there is no opportunity.

My wife's uncle did not want a celebration when he passed. He is not alone in these thoughts. But when I die, I hope my life is celebrated for being full and joyful. When I pass, I hope I never said "no" to happiness. I hope the regrets are limited and the rewards are full. So far, so good.

If you would like to learn more about franchising, please contact me. There is never any obligation – I understand you are learning, not buying. Think about it this way - what have you got to loose and what do you have to gain?

I Wish You the Very Best of Success and Happiness in Life!

❧

About the Author

Rich Greer

Rich has been in franchising since 1990, a successful franchisee in two separate systems. By growing his businesses from start-up to being included in the top 2% of revenue in both systems Rich was awarded several prestigious quality and sales awards along the way.

In 2009 Rich sold his businesses and felt a sense of duty to give back to franchising by using his 30 years' franchise experience. He became a franchise broker. As an award winning franchise broker Rich has helped hundreds of people find the franchise of their dreams. Many times Rich's clients have called and thanked him for helping them. Rich has developed a process to analyze his client's business, financial and lifestyle goals and industries of preference to present franchises that hold great promise. Best of all - Rich's services are free to his clients.

About the Author

Rich holds an MBA from Regis University in Denver Colorado as well as the prestigious Certified Franchise Broker certification and the Certified Franchise Consultant certification. Rich is also an Eagle Scout, as is his son Michael (remember him from the introduction?).

Please feel free to reach out for more information about franchising. I promise – no obligations on your part at all.

Rich Greer's email: Rich.Greer@NationsFranchiseSource.com

www.ingramcontent.com/pod-product-compliance
Lightning Source LLC
Chambersburg PA
CBHW021415210526
45463CB00001B/381